LUCENT LIBRARY *of* HISTORICAL ERAS

A LIFE FOR GOD:
THE MEDIEVAL MONASTERY

Titles in the series include:

LUCENT LIBRARY ◆of◆ HISTORICAL ERAS

A LIFE FOR GOD:
THE MEDIEVAL MONASTERY

WILLIAM W. LACE

LUCENT BOOKS

An imprint of Thomson Gale, a part of The Thomson Corporation

THOMSON

GALE

Detroit • New York • San Francisco • San Diego • New Haven, Conn. • Waterville, Maine • London • Munich

LIBRARY OF CONGRESS CATALOGING-IN-PUBLICATION DATA

Lace, William W.
    A life for God : the medieval monastery / by William W. Lace.
        p. cm. — (The Lucent library of historical eras. Middle Ages)
    Includes bibliographical references and index.
    ISBN 1-59018-847-0 (hard cover : alk. paper) 1. Monastic and religious life—History—Middle Ages, 600-1500. I. Title. II. Series.
BX2435.L33 2006
271.009'02—dc22
                                                              2005029067

Printed in China

Contents

Foreword

Looking back from the vantage point of the present, history can be viewed as a myriad of intertwining roads paved by human events. Some paths stand out—broad highways whose mileposts, even from a distance of centuries, are clear. The events that propelled the rise to power of Germany's Third Reich, its role in World War II, and its eventual demise, for example, are well defined and documented.

Other roads are less distinct, their route sometimes hidden from view. Modern legislatures may have developed from old tribal councils, for example, but the links between them are indistinct in places, open to discussion and interpretation.

The architecture of civilization—law, religion, art, science, and government—as well as the more everyday aspects of our culture—what we eat, what we wear—all developed along the historical roads and byways. In that progression can be traced every facet of modern life.

A broad look back along these roads reveals that many paths—though of vastly different character—seem to converge at a few critical junctions. These intersections are those great historical eras that echo over the long, steady course of human history, extending beyond the past and into the present.

These epic periods of time are the focus of Lucent's Library of Historical Eras. They shine through the mists of history like beacons, illuminated by a burst of creativity that propels events forward—so bright that we, from thousands of years away, can clearly see the chain of events leading to the present.

Each Lucent Library of Historical Eras consists of a set of books that highlight various aspects of these major eras. For example, the Elizabethan England library features volumes on Queen Elizabeth I and her court, Elizabethan theater, the great playwrights, and everyday life in Elizabethan London.

The mini-library approach allows for the division of each era into its most significant and most interesting parts and the exploration of those parts in depth. Also, social and cultural trends as well as illustrative documents and eyewitness accounts can be prominently featured in individual volumes.

Lucent's Library of Historical Eras presents a wealth of information to young readers. The lively narrative, fully documented primary and secondary source quotations, maps, photographs, sidebars, and annotated bibliographies serve as launching points for class discussion and further research.

In studying the great historical eras, students also develop a better understanding of our own times. What we learn from the past and how we apply it in the present may shape the future and may determine whether our era will be a guiding light to those traveling future roads.

Introduction

THE RISE OF THE MONASTIC MOVEMENT

Thousands of men and women throughout history have begun their search for the spirit within them by retreating from the world around them. Their spiritual quest has led them to lives in deserts, caves, atop pillars, in trees, and in silent, secluded cells. They gave their lives to God, but in the process they also gave the Middle Ages much of its flavor as well as leaving a priceless legacy of art, literature, and learning.

The notion of monasticism, from the Greek *monos*, meaning "alone," did not arise in the Middle Ages, nor was it unique to Christianity. Buddhist monks and nuns date from about 1500 B.C., and both Jesus and John the Baptist, key figures in Christianity, are thought to have been influenced by the Essenes, a group of Jewish ascetics who withdrew into the desert in about 150 B.C. to await the end of the world that they thought was imminent. It was Christian monasticism, how-

ever, starting in the third century after Jesus's death, that was to leave its imprint so vividly on Western civilization.

Anthony of the Desert and his disciple Pachomius are generally considered the founders of Christian monasticism. In A.D. 271, the young Anthony heard a sermon on Jesus's commandment (Matthew 19:21), "If you would be perfect, go, sell what you possess and give to the poor, and you will have treasure in heaven; and come, follow me." Thus inspired, Anthony sold all his possessions and, in order to distance himself further from worldly matters, sought a life of solitude and chastity, first in a small hut outside his Egyptian village and later in a vacant tomb nearby.

Complete solitude, however, eluded Anthony. Others were drawn by his sanctity, seeking him out to give them spiritual comfort. Gradually, a small colony of hermits grew up around him, coming together only rarely, but acknowledging him as their abbot, or leader.

Pachomius

Pachomius took the next step. Following Anthony's example, he joined a colony of hermits along the banks of the Nile River but soon demonstrated administrative abilities that equaled his piety. He organ-ized the monks into a community and added obedience to the general requirements of poverty and chastity as practiced by St. Anthony.

The great stimulus for the spread of monasticism, however, occurred in about 330 when the emperor Constantine made Christianity the favored religion of the Roman Empire. Suddenly, rather than being a persecuted minority, Christians

This fifteenth-century painting depicts a band of demons trying to tempt Anthony of the Desert, regarded as one of the founders of monasticism.

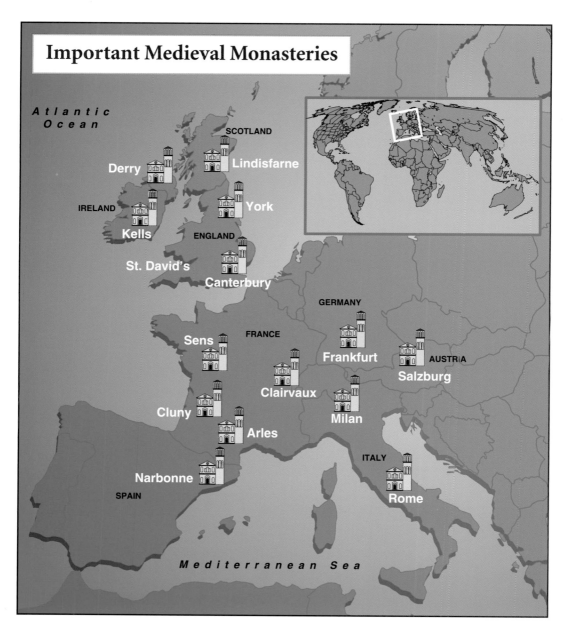

Important Medieval Monasteries

Atlantic
Ocean

SCOTLAND

Derry

Lindisfarne

IRELAND

York

Kells

ENGLAND

St. David's

Canterbury

GERMANY

FRANCE

Sens

Frankfurt

AUSTRIA

Salzburg

Clairvaux

Cluny

Milan

Arles

ITALY

Narbonne

SPAIN

Rome

Mediterranean Sea

were in positions of power. Many people, however, felt that the church was losing in piety what it had gained in prestige. Increasingly, by joining monasteries, they sought to return to what they believed Jesus had taught.

Much of the expansion was eastward from Egypt toward Constantinople due to the efforts of St. Basil (329–379), who devoted much of his energy to the development of a style of monasticism different from that of the Egyptian ascetics. In addition to prayer, chastity, and obedience, Basil thought monks should lead useful lives of service in the community, operating hospitals, orphanages, and schools.

Westward Expansion

Compared to its eastward spread, the expansion of monasticism westward was much more haphazard. In the words of historian David Knowles, it spread "gradually and sporadically as a plant spreads from seeds that are blown abroad."[1] Houses for both men and women were founded throughout North Africa, Italy, and Gaul (modern France). They did not adopt a common rule, or set of regulations, as did houses in the East, but followed the leads of their individual founders and abbots.

Such diversity gradually gave way starting in the 500s when Abbot Benedict of Nursia wrote his famous *Rule*, an intensely practical guide for monastic living. So practical and appealing was this guide, in fact, that it eventually was almost univer-

sally adopted throughout Western Europe and its practitioners became known as Benedictines.

Western monasticism would endure a long cycle of trouble and triumph throughout the Middle Ages. It survived the turbulent centuries of barbarian invasions that followed the fall of Rome in 476, prospered under Emperor Charlemagne in the 800s, suffered during the breakup of Charlemagne's empire, and finally enjoyed a full flowering between 1050 and 1200.

The dominance of monasticism and, indeed, of the entire Roman Catholic Church was in many ways confined to the Middle Ages. That dominance was eventually swept away by the Renaissance and, later, by the Protestant Reformation. Monks and nuns would never again be seen as lighting the way for the rest of humankind. However, the light they held for so long, one that illuminated many dark corners of civilization, is not only reflected in their legacy, but also woven throughout the rich tapestry that is the Middle Ages.

Chapter One

THE SEARCH FOR THE SOUL

In about A.D. 385 a young intellectual named Aurelius Augustinius, the future St. Augustine of Hippo, could no longer deny that his life had been wasted in sin and idleness. Later, in his *Confessions*, he wrote that God "didst set me face to face with myself, that I might see how ugly I was, and how crooked and sordid, bespotted and ulcerous. And I looked and I loathed myself; but whither to fly from myself I could not discover."[2]

Augustine's torment continued until he ran across a passage from St. Paul's letter to the Romans (13:14) urging them to "put on the Lord Jesus Christ, and make no provision for the flesh, to gratify its desires." Instantly, Augustine wrote, "there was infused in my heart something like the light of full certainty and all the gloom of doubt vanished away."[3] Ever since, many millions of people in spiritual crisis have had the same revelation as St. Augustine. They have come face to face with themselves and have resolved to change what they see reflected there, to put their old lives behind them and to "put on" the monastic life.

One of the primary motives for monasticism, then, has been self-discovery, based on the presumption that the secular world contains too many distractions for such discovery to take place. Internal barriers—sin, pride, ignorance—have also been perceived as interfering with the search for self, and these can be overcome only by living the strict, rigorous lifestyle of a monk or nun. Such determination was, and is, renewed in the Benedictines' annual vow near the time of Easter: "I do reject sin, so as to live in the freedom of God's children. I do reject the glamour of evil, and refuse to be mastered by sin. I do reject Satan, father of sin and prince of darkness, in order to pass to the Father."[4]

Search for Perfection

In addition to self-discovery, men and women sought a monastic life in order to come as close as possible to spiritual perfection. Sometimes this involved a rejection—often extreme—of physical needs. Especially in the early centuries, monks would try to exist on as little food as possible and suffer all discomforts possible, punishing their bodies in an effort to uplift their spirits.

Sometimes the quest for perfection through denial led to a paradox in which monks took great pride in their humility, thus counteracting what they had hoped to achieve. As a present-day abbot, Father John Eudes Bamberger of the Abbey of the Genesee in New York, writes

In this medieval Italian fresco, two monks sitting outside their monastery discuss a passage from the Bible.

of extreme asceticism, "Pride is so inter-mingled with this approach to perfection that what sets out to be virtue soon develops into an obstacle to union with God by subtly inculcating a false pride."[5]

Self-discovery and the search for perfection, however, were only means to the ultimate goals of redemption and salvation. Monks and nuns thought that the monastic life—which involved prayer, good works, and the rejection of worldly pleasures—would help them attain redemption, or forgiveness of their sins. From redemption, they hoped, would come salvation, which in the Christian sense means the resurrection of the body after death to eternal life with God.

Benedict, in fact, likened a monastery to a "school for the Lord's service." In his *Rule*, he compared the monastic life to the hard road and narrow gate that, according to the Gospel of Matthew (7:14), Jesus had said were required for salvation. Benedict cautioned monks to

A Hermit's Abode

The earliest monks were hermits who took up solitary lives in the Egyptian desert. Eventually, however, they could not escape the attention of would-be disciples. This description of how St. Hilarion lived is contained in a biography by St. Jerome.

There is a high and rocky mountain extending for about a mile, with gushing springs amongst its spurs, the waters of which are partly absorbed by the sand, partly flow towards the plain and gradually form a stream shaded on either side by countless palms which lend much pleasantness and charm to the place. Here the old man might be seen pacing to and fro with the disciples of blessed Antony. Here, so they said, Antony himself used to sing, pray, work, and rest when weary. Those vines and shrubs were planted by his own hand: that garden bed was his own design. This pool for watering the garden was made by him after much toil. That hoe was handled by him for many years. Hilarion would lie upon the saint's bed and as though it were still warm would affectionately kiss it. The cell was square, its sides measuring no more than the length of a sleeping man. Moreover on the lofty mountaintop, the ascent of which was by a zig-zag path very difficult, were to be seen two cells of the same dimensions, in which he stayed when he escaped from the crowds of visitors or the company of his disciples. These were cut out of the live rock and were only furnished with doors.

St. Jerome, "Life of St. Hilarion." *Catholic Encyclopedia.* www.newadvent.org/fathers/3003.htm

A Gothic king kneels before St. Benedict, as the ruler asks the monk for his blessing.

persevere in their chosen path so that "continuing in the monastery in his teaching until death, through patience we are made partakers in Christ's passion, in order that we may merit to be companions in His kingdom."[6]

"Good Works"

Many people, however, did not become monks and nuns for individually spiritual reasons, but to advance the work of the church and to help humankind. They believed that forces of evil actively worked against God's will and that it was their duty to battle those forces. Augustine wrote, "O servants of God, soldiers of Christ! . . . Does not your heart wax hot within you, and in your meditation a fire kindle, that these men's evil works ye should pursue with good works, that ye should cut off from them occasion of a foul trafficking, by which your estimation is hurt, and a stumbling-block put before the weak?"[7]

The "good works" Augustine referred to constituted yet another attraction of monasteries. Monks served as counselors to kings, and some monasteries became international centers for religious training.

They preserved and disseminated literature and learning, furnished a place of refuge and hospitality to travelers and the poor, and cared for the sick. In a way, good works came to define monasticism. As a modern definition of Benedictine spirituality puts it, "Through constant attention to the needs of others we give up our own comfort so that someone else may find the true comfort of Christ.... Indeed only by such faithful service are we truly free to use all things for God's glory rather than our own selfish purposes."[8]

People of Wealth

With such a wide range of reasons why men and women chose the monastic life, it might be assumed that monks and nuns came from a wide range of social classes. Such, however, was not generally the case. In the Early Middle Ages, most of those who retreated to the desert as hermits or who accepted a life of poverty in a monastery were people of some wealth who felt that their material well-being put their spiritual health at risk. Athanasius, in his fourth-century biography of Anthony, writes that Anthony gave away all his possessions "that they should be no more a clog upon himself and his sister."[9]

This desire for poverty was frequently the result of religious zeal. The future St. Hilarion was, according to his biographer, St. Jerome, "a believer in the Lord Jesus, and took no delight in the madness of the circus, the blood of the arena, the excesses of the theatre: his whole pleasure was in the assemblies of the Church."[10] The Englishman Boniface is supposed to have decided at the age of four to become a monk and, even at that age, "had subdued the flesh to the spirit and meditated on the things that are eternal rather than on those that are temporal."[11]

Sometimes a dramatic conversion or vision influenced the decision to renounce wealth and become a monk or nun. St. Francis of Assisi, according to a biography written by Thomas of Celano in 1181, was praying before a figure of Jesus on the cross:

> Devoutly lying prostrate before the crucifix, stirred by unusual visitations, he found he was different than when he had entered. While he was in this affected state, something absolutely unheard-of occurred. The crucifix moved its lips and began to speak. "Francis," it said, calling him by name, "go and repair my house, which, as you see, is completely destroyed." Francis was stupefied and nearly deranged by this speech. He prepared to obey, surrendering himself completely to the project.[12]

Worldly Motives

The decision to become a monk or nun sometimes was driven as much by ambition as by devotion. Young men from poor families frequently saw the church as their only path of advancement. While such men could not hope to achieve power or influence through military

Endowments

Many wealthy noblemen in the Middle Ages sought to ensure their entry into heaven by contributing to monastic orders while on earth. Such a man was William the Pious, founder of the great Benedictine monastery at Cluny. In this portion of his will, he gave the manor of Cluny to become a monastery.

It is manifest to all who rightly consider, and God's Providence doth so counsel all rich men, that it is in their power to earn everlasting rewards by a good use of those things which are now in their transitory possession. . . . Therefore I William by God's grace, Count and Duke, carefully weighing these things, and willing to provide for mine own salvation while there is yet time . . . grant of mine own free will, to the holy Apostles Peter and Paul, certain of my rightful possessions; namely Cluny, with its court and manor, and its chapel in honour of Mary the holy Mother of God and St. Peter, Chief of the Apostles, together with all that pertaineth unto the said village. . . . On this condition, that a regular monastery be built at Cluny in honour of the holy Apostles Peter and Paul, wherein monks shall possess, hold, have, and ordain these possessions aforesaid, to all time.

Quoted in George Gordon Coulton, *Life in the Middle Ages.* Cambridge, UK: Cambridge University Press, 1967, book III.

prowess or land ownership, they could do so in a monastery on their own merits.

This pattern did not hold true for women. Only rarely did a woman from a poor family become a nun. More often would-be nuns were unmarried women from upper-class families who found the life of a nun the only alternative to marriage. Some were widows who donated property in exchange for entrance into a convent.

Often, however, the decision to join a monastery or convent was made not by the prospective monk or nun, but by his or her family. It was not uncommon for families to "give" a child to God. Such children were called oblates, from a form of the Latin verb meaning "to offer." The gift might occur in several ways. Sometimes, a parent had a dream that the child was destined for a religious life. Other children might be given to a monastery if they or some other family member survived a serious illness.

Unwanted Children

Some children, however, were given to a monastery because they were unwanted. Parents might consider a son too unruly

In this page from a thirteenth-century illustrated manuscript, wealthy parents leave their son with a monk outside a monastery.

or a daughter unmarriageable for some reason. A poor family might simply have too many mouths to feed. Illegitimate children were sometimes left at the gates of monasteries so that the mother did not have to face the public shame of having borne a baby out of wedlock.

For the most part, however, oblates came from well-to-do families. This was because the families were expected to make a significant monetary contribution to the monastery at the time a child was turned over. The parents of Oderic Vitalis, for instance, paid thirty marks (the equivalent today of about $125 and at the time a significant sum) to the monastery of St. Evroul.

For Oderic, and very likely for many other oblates, parting from their families was difficult. In an appendix to his *Ecclesiastical History of England and Normandy*, he recalled leaving England and entering a monastery in France:

> My father, Odeler, wept as he gave me, a weeping child, to Rainald the monk, and sent me into exile for your [Jesus's] love—nor ever after saw me. A small boy did not presume to contradict his father, but I obeyed him in all things, since he promised me that I should possess paradise with the innocent. And so I left my country, my parents, all my kindred and my friends.[13]

Indeed, becoming a monk or nun, whether in another country or not, meant an almost total separation from one's previous life. Contact with friends or visits from family members were not encouraged, at least in the monasteries of Western Europe.

Entering a monastery, whether as an adult or child, did not make one a monk or nun. Several steps were necessary before newcomers could become full-fledged members of the community. First they had to spend a year or more as a novice, during which they were to learn and obey the rules of the order. At the same time, they judged for themselves and were judged by others as to their fitness for monastic life.

"Hard and Rugged Things"

Some newcomers doubtless thought that a life of quiet solitude would also be one of ease. To dispel this notion, wrote St. Benedict, a man seeking to become a monk should be admitted to the monastery only after repeated requests and then only to guests' quarters. If, after a few days' stay, he still wishes to become a novice, "Let him be shown all the hard and rugged things through which we pass on to God."[14]

The monk assigned to both guide and test the prospective monk was the novice master, usually one of the oldest, most experienced members of the community. It was his task, wrote medieval chronicler Walter Daniel, to make sure that his charges were "worthy vessels of God and acceptable to the Order."[15] He observed them closely, seeking to learn, first, if they were truly fit for life as a monk and, second, whether they were seeking to avoid something—debts, military service, the law, for example—rather than seeking to find God.

The vows taken by monks varied according to the order, but all incorporated three basic concepts—obedience, poverty, and chastity. Also incorporated into the vows were promises to remain in the monastic community and to seek additional spiritual growth. A present-day monk, the Reverend Brian Taylor, describes the Benedictine vow, which has remained virtually unchanged over the centuries, this way:

> The Benedictine vow asks three things: first, for the monk to remain in one monastery for the rest of his or her life: this is called *stability*. Secondly, it asks for *obedience*, which means that the monk lives a certain lifestyle, according to the Rule of St.

Advice to a Nun

When St. Eustochium took her vows as a nun in A.D. 384, St. Jerome, who was a friend of her family, wrote a lengthy letter giving her advice on how to conduct herself in almost all aspects of life.

Do not court the company of married ladies or visit the houses of the highborn. Do not look too often on the life which you despised to become a virgin. Women of the world, you know, plume themselves because their husbands are on the bench [serving as judges] or in other high positions. . . . Let your companions be women pale and thin with fasting, and approved by their years and conduct. . . . Be subject to your parents, imitating the example of your spouse [Jesus]. Rarely go abroad, and if you wish to seek the aid of the martyrs, seek it in your own chamber. . . . Take food in moderation, and never overload your stomach. For many women, while temperate as regards wine, are intemperate in the use of food. When you rise at night to pray, let your breath be that of an empty and not that of an overfull stomach. Read often, learn all that you can. Let sleep overcome you, the roll [of bread] still in your hands; when your head falls, let it be on the sacred page. Let your fasts be of daily occurrence and your refreshment such as avoids satiety . . . If ever you feel the outward man sighing for the flower of youth, and if, as you lie on your couch after a meal, you are excited by the alluring train of sensual desires; then seize the shield of faith, for it alone can quench the fiery darts of the devil.

St. Jerome, "To Eustochium." Internet History Sourcebooks Project, Paul Halsall, editor. www.fordham.edu/hal sall/basis/jerome-letter22.html.

St. Francis of Assisi is depicted in this painting with tonsured hair and wearing a habit.

Benedict. Thirdly, it asks one to commit to ongoing change and growth, called *conversion of life.* So stability, obedience, conversion of life, these three: but it's all one life, one vow—just as God is three persons in one unity of Being.[16]

Habits and Tonsures

Once the monks and nuns took their final vows, they were clothed in the distinctive habit, or clothing, of the order. The Benedictines' robes were black, giving rise to the term "black monks." The Cistercians were "white monks" and the Franciscans "gray friars" for similar reasons. Nuns' orders also had characteristic dress, the most distinctive part of which was the wimple, or head covering.

Men were given distinctive haircuts known as tonsures. The most common form in Europe was to shave the crown of the head, leaving a circular fringe. The Celtic monks of Ireland and Scotland shaved a crescent of hair from the front of the head from ear to ear, leaving the back. Some orders in the East shaved the entire head. Nuns normally had their hair either shaved completely off or cut very short, depending on the order, but the head was covered by the wimple.

Thus, symbolically as well as in reality, monks and nuns put aside their old life and joined a new family. Just as in their old existence, however, they would have an authority figure to obey, work to do, and "sisters or brothers" to get along with.

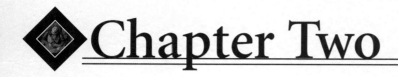

Chapter Two

A Life of Obedience

From the earliest days, when the hermits in the deserts of Egypt began to gather into small communities, obedience has been one of the three foundations of monasticism, the other two being chastity and poverty. As Benedict wrote sometime about A.D. 530 in his *Rule*, "The first degree of humility is obedience without delay."[17]

Benedict's *Rule* revolutionized monastic life in Western Europe. The book is fairly short and organized into concise chapters. While calling for strict obedience and a high degree of spirituality, it is a practical document that is flexible and moderate in its physical demands, making allowances for age, infirmity, and illness. This was in contrast to earlier monastic rules, such as that of Pachomias, a former soldier who required unbending obedience and prescribed harsh punishments for offenders. "Benedict's monastery," writes historian David Knowles, "is neither a penitentiary nor a school of ascetic mountaineering, but a family, a home of those seeking God."[18] Thus it is that a discussion of monastic obedience in the Middle Ages is really a description of life in a Benedictine house.

Obedience was owed, of course, to God's law as set down in the Bible and to man's law as prescribed by the rule of the order. On a more immediate and practical level, however, obedience was owed to one's superiors, especially the abbot or abbess. Monks and nuns were to obey orders instantaneously and without question. Here, however, the military and spiritual aspects of monasticism differed. Obedience was to come not from respect for the law or fear of punishment, but from the heart—from a fervent desire to emulate Jesus to every extent possible. Augustine of Hippo, in his rule written for a convent of nuns, said that it was not God's purpose that they be "as slaves living under the law but as men [or women] living in freedom under grace."[19]

Limits on Freedom

That freedom, however, was extremely limited—not so much by the rules under which monks and nuns lived, but by their zeal in obeying them. Their purpose in that zeal was nothing less than attaining a state of grace—to earn a place beside Jesus in heaven. And Benedict cautioned those who became monks and nuns that if his *Rule* "dictateth anything that turneth out somewhat stringent, do not at once fly in dismay from the way of salvation, the beginning of which cannot but be narrow."[20]

The chief enemy of obedience, in the monastic view, was pride, and the chief weapon against pride was humility. Benedict went to great lengths in the *Rule* to explain this, detailing twelve separate "degrees" of humility. Monks and nuns should be silent insofar as possible, refrain from laughter, and do nothing

Monks, like these pictured reading Scripture outside their mountaintop monastery, applied themselves to intensive biblical study in order to achieve a state of grace.

Avoiding Temptation

One of the basic vows that monks and nuns had to obey was that of chastity. They best avoided temptation by avoiding contact with the opposite sex. In this account by an anonymous chronicler, however, a monk and nun placed themselves in close proximity and then took extraordinary steps to stay apart.

Never, as I think, did the cunning fiend send sharper temptations, or set more snares, for any man [a monk named Roger]; but he, armed with the virtue of the Cross, conquered the first by God's grace, and avoided the second with the utmost discretion. . . . His devoted disciple was the Blessed Christina. . . . Yet he never consented to see the virgin's face, though for four years and more she was shut up in his cell. Now there was a building adjoining the oratory of the said Roger, with which it made an angle. This [angle] having a board before it, might so be concealed as to lead the outside beholder to suppose that no man was in this space. . . . In this prison Roger placed the joyful Christina, and set for a door a proper oaken plank which was so heavy that the anchoress [Christina] could by no means move it either to or fro. Here the handmaiden of Christ sat crouching on the hard cold stone until Roger's death, unknown to the five hermits and to all who dwelt together with Roger. Oh, what discomforts she there endured from heat and cold, hunger and thirst, and daily fasting.

Quoted in George Gordon Coulton, *Life in the Middle Ages.* Cambridge, UK: Cambridge University Press, 1967, book I.

apart from what is called for in the *Rule* or ordered by their superiors. They should be "content with the meanest and worst of everything"[21] and, when they have evil thoughts, confess them.

Finally, like obedience, humility should be both internal and external. The humble monk "in his innermost soul believeth that he is the lowest and vilest of men."[22] Such beliefs are to be demonstrated outwardly by going about at all times with head bowed and eyes on the ground.

The medieval monastery or convent was thus a solemn, silent place. Even in the comparatively lenient Benedictine monasteries, private speech, which did not include prayer or reading aloud from scripture or other sacred texts, was supposed to be "for good and holy and edifying discourse."[23] Other orders, such as the Carthusians and the Cistercians, imposed a rule of silence that prohibited almost all speech.

Monastic Meals

Just as speech was kept to a minimum for the good of the soul, food was seen as something to nourish the body but not necessarily to be enjoyed. Ordinary monks were doubtless happy to see guests arrive, for their abbot might allow more interesting food to be served. Otherwise, daily fare was plain, but plentiful. St. Benedict called for two types of cooked dishes to be available in addition to bread and wine. These would usually come from among cheese, eggs, or preserved vegetables. Fresh fruit or vegetables from the monastery gardens or orchards might constitute a third dish.

Fish and poultry were served only rarely, usually on feast days. In keeping with their vow of poverty, the monks, except for those who were weak or ill,

A table of Benedictine monks sits in silence as they share a modest meal of fish, bread, and vegetables.

were prohibited from eating beef or mutton—what the *Rule* called "the flesh of four-footed animals."[24] As soon as a monk had regained his strength or health, he was supposed to return to the usual diet—a rule that may have acted to lengthen some recovery times.

Benedict's personal opinion was that it was improper for a monk to drink wine, but he was a realistic man with a firm grasp of human nature. He knew that "monks in our times cannot be persuaded" to abstain from wine, so he instead sought to limit its use.[25] He reckoned that one hermia—about 10 ounces (0.3l)—of wine per day would be sufficient, but allowed for more if circumstances, such as the amount of work or excessive heat, required more.

The number of meals each day depended on the season of the year and the amount of work to be done. St. Benedict thought that a single main meal served at about 3 P.M. was sufficient during colder months, although more might be provided for the sick, the very young, and the very old. In the summer, when days were longer and there was much more work to be done in the fields or with livestock, both a noontime and evening meal were served.

Whenever possible, monks ate together in a large room known as the refectory, although novices and oblates sometimes dined separately. The monks ate in silence unbroken except for the voice of the person assigned to read scripture during the meals that week. The "weekly readers" could fortify themselves beforehand with a little bread and wine, and then take their meals afterward with the kitchen servers.

All the monks took turns serving in the kitchen, except in large, wealthy monasteries that had lay brothers—those not intending to take permanent vows—who acted as servants. The servers had various functions in addition to those involving food. One was to wash the feet of everyone, just as Jesus was believed to have washed the feet of his disciples before the Last Supper. Another was to wash the towels with which the monks dried their hands and feet. Yet another was to collect utensils from the cellarer, the monk in charge of the kitchen and pantry, and make sure they were cleaned and returned.

Monastic Sleeping Arrangements

Bedtime, like mealtime, depended on the time of year. In the winter, especially in northern latitudes where days were very short, monks spent about two hours after their single meal in prayer and reading and were in bed shortly after 5 P.M. In the summer, when there was more daylight for work, bedtime was at about 8 P.M.

Monks generally slept in the same room—the dormitory—although novices and oblates sometimes had a separate room. Larger houses might have more than one dormitory. Occasionally, as with the Trappists, monks slept in individual rooms known as cells. Cells were also the rule rather than the exception in convents.

Pursuing Poverty

Many monks, having taken vows of poverty, seemed to have a real fear of money and took pains not to let it tempt them. In his letter to St. Eustochium, St. Jerome told of how one group of monks avoided such temptation.

A brother, more thrifty than covetous, and ignorant that the Lord had been sold for thirty pieces of silver, left behind him at his death a hundred pieces of money which he had earned by weaving linen. As there were about five thousand monks in the neighborhood, living in as many separate cells, a council was held as to what should be done. Some said that the coins should be distributed among the poor; others that they should be given to the church, while others were for sending them back to the relatives of the deceased. However, Macarius, Pambo, Isidore and the rest of those called fathers, speaking by the Spirit, decided that they should be interred with their owner, with the words: "Thy money perish with thee." Nor was this too harsh a decision; for so great fear has fallen upon all throughout Egypt, that it is now a crime to leave after one a single shilling.

St. Jerome, "To Eustochium." Internet History Sourcebooks Project, Paul Halsall, editor. www.fordham. edu/hal sall/basis/jerome-letter22.html.

Monks used little in the way of bedding and, in fact, had no beds, sleeping instead on the dormitory floor. Benedict wrote that each person should have a straw mattress, blanket, coverlet, and pillow. He added that the monks' bedding should be examined frequently by the abbot, not to check for cleanliness, but to see if any personal possessions had been hidden.

Possessions, Poverty, and Punishment

Possessions, or lack of them, constituted one of Benedict's favorite themes. Poverty, in his view, was an essential ingredient of obedience. Personal ownership, he wrote, was "a vice [that] must by all means be cut out in the monastery by the very root . . . since monks are allowed to have neither their bodies nor their wills in their own power."[26]

Obedience to the rule of poverty, then, meant that everything the monks or nuns had was owned by the monastery and given to them by their superior. Included were clothing, bedding, books, and all tools or implements. "Let everything necessary be given by the Abbot," Benedict wrote, "namely, cowl, tunic, stockings, shoes, girdle [belt], knife, pen, needle, towel, writing tablet; that all pretence of want may be removed."[27]

Should the monk be found to have anything other than what he had been permitted to use, he was to "fall under the severest discipline."[28] Under the Benedictine *Rule*, this was excommunication, but not in the sense commonly understood today—expulsion from the church. Benedict's excommunication, covered in five chapters of his *Rule*, consisted of several degrees of punishment according to the gravity of the offense. For minor infractions, such as unauthorized speech, the guilty party might be prohibited from taking meals with the others. Repeated or more serious infractions, such as having personal possessions, might mean that no one could associate with an offender. In addition, the offender's food ration might be cut. If such chastisement did not bring results, corporal punishment—whipping—was the next step. If the monk still did not repent or if he tried

This photograph depicts adjoining dormitory cells in an Italian convent, both of which have frescoes painted on the walls.

Monastic Punishment

In this excerpt from a twelfth-century document, a monk describes his punishment. His offense had been returning to his bed to retrieve a book while wearing the wrong colored tunic.

The Father [abbot] gave the horrid hateful doom that I should forthwith be stripped of my garments. Hard was the sentence, yet, willy-nilly, I obeyed; for God Himself hath bidden that the condemned man should obey his angry judge. Then cleave I naked to the ground; upon me they begin to wreak their heavy vengeance; I am scourged, poor wretch, until I almost give up the ghost in my misery. The two stout arms that smite upon me are ready to fail for weariness. What can I say or do? Nought availeth me; neither cross, nor image [of Jesus] thereon, before whose face I suffered such grievous torment this hour. Who would not marvel that none could be found to pity this poor wretch? Unable to bear the stripes, I cast myself to the ground; tortured and fainting, while my blood flowed on every side. I had given up the ghost, had this wrathe endured but a little long; yea, I had become an unprofitable carcase. But, when my blood began to flow, then the Lord, who heleth all wounds, touched the heart of these butchers, and unnerved their pitiless sinews; wherefore the brethren left me there bruised and scourged to the utmost.

Quoted in George Gordon Coulton, *Life in the Middle Ages*. Cambridge, UK: Cambridge University Press, 1967, book II.

to defend his actions, the abbot was instructed to have the entire community pray for the offender "that the Lord who is all-powerful may work a cure in that brother."[29]

Finally, as a last resort, the offender could be banished from the monastery, but this was not necessarily the end of the story. Benedict provided that if a banished brother repented, he could be welcomed back—not just once, but twice. If he was banished a third time, however, it was for good.

The person who enforced obedience by meting out punishments—the abbot or abbess—was not exempt from the rules. Just as the monk was answerable to the abbot, Benedict wrote, the abbot was answerable to God. Accordingly, "Let the Abbot always bear in mind that he must give an account in the dread judgment of God of both his own teaching and of the obedience of his disciples. And let the Abbot know that whatever lack of profit the master of the house shall find in the sheep, will be laid to the blame of the shepherd."[30]

Chapter Three

A LIFE OF WORK

A monk's or nun's life might be one of disciplined peace, quiet, prayer, and meditation, but it was not one of ease. Benedict wrote, "Idleness is the enemy of the soul; and therefore the brethren ought to be employed in manual labor at certain times . . . they live by the work of their hands, as did also our forefathers and the Apostles."[31]

This is not to say that prayer and work were considered mutually exclusive. Francis of Assisi agreed with Benedict as to the danger of idleness, but he added that work is of more use than filling time. He told his followers, "The friars to whom God has given the grace of working should work in a spirit of faith and devotion and avoid idleness, which is the enemy of the soul, without however extinguishing the spirit of prayer and devotion, to which every temporal consideration must be subordinate."[32]

So, while there were a few exceptions—notably orders whose only task was per-

petual prayer—monastic lives were a complementary balance of the spiritual and the physical. Everyone had specialized tasks to perform in addition to mundane assignments such as serving in the kitchen and in the refectory.

Specialized Jobs in Benedict's *Rule*

Some of the work involved operating the monastery or convent itself. Benedict realized that even the small monasteries for which he wrote the *Rule*, those with twelve members and an abbot or abbess, needed some division of labor. Accordingly, he specified two specialized jobs—the cellarer and the porter.

The cellarer was in charge of buying and distributing all food and drink that were not produced at the monastery. It was up to him, under the abbot's direction, to decide how much of what kind of food

A monk oversees construction of an abbey in France, while two other monks arrive on the riverbank with supplies.

would be provided to whom. Such responsibility, Benedict wrote, required a monk to be "a wise man, of settled habits, temperate and frugal, not conceited, irritable, resentful, sluggish, or wasteful, but fearing God, who may be as a father to the whole brotherhood."[33] While called on to be frugal, he nevertheless was to be compassionate in allotting food to the elderly or sick.

The monk assigned the second full-time task designated by Benedict—the porter—was to station himself in a small room next to the gate. It was his job to greet anyone who came to the monastery, to be able to answer anyone's question, and to have the wisdom to know who should and should not be admitted.

It was also the porter's duty to know who went out as well as who came in. Benedict urged that all goods be stored, insofar as possible, inside the walls, so that monks would not have to go outside, "because it is not good for their souls."[34] Knowing that the porter himself might be tempted to wander, Benedict called for him to be "a wise old man . . . whose mature age doth not permit him to stray about."[35]

There was one other official mentioned in Benedict's rule. Realizing that a monastery could grow so large that the abbot would need help in governing, Benedict thus made allowances, although reluctantly, for a prior or prioress, a second in command. However, Benedict saw the danger of the prior thinking of himself as a second abbot, especially in cases in which a bishop had appointed both men. A much better solution, he thought, was for any extra administrative duties to be distributed among several monks known as deans.

Other Specialized Jobs

Medieval monasteries and convents did, indeed, grow large. As they grew, so did the need for more specific jobs within them. When houses grew wealthy enough to give alms, or contributions, instead of only receiving them, the monk in charge was the almoner. He was to look among those living outside the monastery, searching out the sick and poor, and, with humility and kindness, give them the best of what the monks produced.

Another by-product of growth was an increase in the number of people seeking to become monks and nuns. The novice master or mistress was in charge of their education and their daily activities, no matter how insignificant. Lanfranc, archbishop of Canterbury in England in the eleventh century, specified that novices "should not speak with one another unless a master is present to hear what is said."[36] It was important that the novice master learn the hearts of those he supervised since it was to him that the abbot turned for an opinion on whether the novice was ready to profess vows.

As the monastic movement grew, worship services at monasteries became more elaborate. Abbots and priests celebrating mass often wore rich robes, especially on occasions such as Easter. The plates and cups in which the bread and wine of communion were served evolved from wood into precious metals, sometimes studded with jewels. So involved did the service become that a monk—the sacrist—was assigned to look after everything necessary to celebrate it. Similarly, the simple chants of early monks and nuns grew so elaborate that a choir master became necessary.

The more elaborate the monastic house, the more specialized the occupations required, especially if the monastery or convent became a center of learning or healing. The great Benedictine houses of Cluny and Bec in

A Monastic Rivalry

As monasteries grew in size throughout the Middle Ages, some found themselves too close for comfort. When the monks of Dijon and St.-Seine in France quarreled violently over property rights, Pope Innocent II had to intervene, as shown in his letter written in 1134.

Bishop Innocent [II], servant of the servants of God, to Hugh [II] the illustrious Duke of Burgundy, health and his Apostolic benediction. The controversy which hath long raged between our sons Herbert Abbot of Dijon and the monks of St-Seine hath now been decided by the prudent discretion of our dear brother Stephen, Abbot of Cîteaux, to whose wisdom we committed the case to be concluded by way of justice or of concord. But the aforesaid monks, intoxicated with the spirit of pride, have not only neglected to keep the agreement prescribed by this our brother aforesaid, but have done the flat contrary. For, invading a certain manor pertaining to St-Étienne [de Dijon], they poured forth the wine of the brethren of that monastery, broke the wine-casks, and despoiled the whole manor both of its beasts and of its other goods. This doth the more grievously affect us, insomuch as we have heard that these things have been done under cover of thy favour. . . . wherefore we command thy nobility to cause the aforesaid concord, made by this wise and careful man, to be observed; and to take all care that the said abbot be no more molested on this account. Otherwise, we fear lest it be imputed to thee if, being able to hinder this evil, thou hinder it not. Our dear daughter the duchess, thy spouse, we salute and bless in the Lord. Given at our palace of Lateran, June 18 (1134).

Quoted in George Gordon Coulton, *Life in the Middle Ages.* Cambridge, UK: Cambridge University Press, 1967, book IV.

France drew scholars from throughout Europe, and their collections of books were so large as to require librarians to keep track of them. Similarly, monastic houses that included hospitals had monks or nuns skilled in medicine.

Agriculture

The majority of monks and nuns, however, worked not in specialized jobs, but either in agriculture or as artisans—mostly the former. It was inevitable, given the development of monasticism, that monks

A group of Cistercian monks uses sickles to harvest wheat. Because most monasteries were supposed to be self-sufficient, monks needed to grow their own food.

St. Augustine on Work

St. Augustine of Hippo had little patience with monks who wanted to lead a life of prayer and contemplation without any kind of manual labor. This criticism, titled "On the Work of Monks," was written in 401.

For what these men are about, who will not do bodily work, to what thing they give up their time, I should like to know. "To prayers," say they, "and psalms, and reading, and the word of God." A holy life, unquestionably, and in sweetness of Christ worthy of praise; but then, if from these we are not to be called off, neither must we eat, nor our daily viands themselves be prepared, that they may be put before us and taken. . . . For one single prayer of one who obeyeth is sooner heard than ten thousand of a despiser. As for divine songs, however, they can easily, even while working with their hands, say them, and like as rowers with a boat-song, so with godly melody cheer up their very toil. . . . What then hinders a servant of God while working with his hands to meditate in the law of the Lord, and sing unto the Name of the Lord Most High? provided, of course, that to learn what he may by memory rehearse, he have times set apart. For to this end also those good works of the faithful ought not to be lacking, for resource of making up what is necessary, that the hours which are so taken up in storing of the mind that those bodily works cannot be carried on, may not oppress with want.

St. Augustine of Hippo, "On the Work of Monks," translated by Rev. H. Browne. *Catholic Encyclopedia*. www.newadvent.org/fathers/1314.htm.

would become farmers. Since their purpose was to withdraw from the world, they needed to be self-sufficient—that is, they needed to produce their own food. They first planted vegetable and herb gardens for their own use and then, thanks to donations of land from the faithful, expanded their efforts to producing grain crops such as wheat, barley, and oats.

The monasteries' landholdings eventually outgrew the monks' ability to operate them, and the monks came to depend on the local population for labor. At first, they employed peasants living on monastic lands. Gradually, however, the monasteries moved toward the use of largely illiterate *conversi*, or lay brothers. The *conversi* were second-class monks. They took a vow of obedience and often lived in the abbey. Their dress was inferior to that of the other monks, however, and they lived and prayed apart. The *conversi* could not become priests and had no vote in the affairs of the monastery.

Agriculture and other practical forms of work were important and necessary to the well-being of the monastery but were mundane enough to be left to lay brothers. However, there was another kind of work—art and architecture—providing a blend of labor and spirituality that probably, although St. Benedict's *Rule* warned against it, gave monks more pride and satisfaction than farm labor did. Throughout the Middle Ages, monks and nuns were able to combine their faith and energies to produce some of Western Europe's greatest treasures.

Illumination

They began with the basic tool of their faith—the Bible. As monasticism spread, so did the need for more copies of the Bible and other sacred texts. Since the printing press had yet to be invented, all books had to be laboriously copied by hand. But a simple rendering of the text was not thought to be enough. If the Bible was the revealed word of God, the thinking went, should it not physically reflect God's glory?

The result was the highly decorative art form known as illumination. Monks decorated the pages of the manuscripts with miniature depictions of Biblical figures, saints, and lavishly ornamented single letters of the alphabet, usually the first letter of the first word on a page, with intertwining branches, leaves, flowers, and exotic animals such as peacocks or even dragons.

Both the copying and illumination of texts demonstrated the patience of monks and nuns. It did not matter that those involved in such a project might not live to see the book completed. They worked not for their own benefit, but for future generations and for the glory of God.

Parchment, Ink, and Pigment

Copying and illuminating were only part of the process. Before the work could begin, parchment, inks, and pigments had to be manufactured. Parchment was made from sheep or goat skins, which were soaked in a solution of quicklime to remove hair, scraped to be as thin as possible, and then lightly sanded on the side to be used so that the inks would stick to the page.

These hand-copied books were meant to last indefinitely. However, ordinary ink made from charcoal soot faded too readily, so a more permanent kind was made by boiling plants high in tannic acid, yielding a brown liquid. A pinch of sulfate or a red-hot iron rod dipped into the liquid turned it black.

Pigments for inks came from a variety of natural sources. Ground-up female cochineal insects yielded bright red, and the shell of the murex, a type of mollusk, was used for crimson. Iron oxide or ochre, liver bile, and saffron furnished yellow. Other minerals used were lapis lazuli (blue), malachite (green), and powdered lead (white).

The glory of illuminated texts, however, was shining swaths of gold, silver, copper,

Monks produced beautifully illuminated manuscripts, such as this fifteenth-century Italian example, as a way to glorify God.

Monastic Wine Merchants

Some monasteries in the Middle Ages were famous for the wine they made. The monks were permitted to drink wine, although not to excess, and to sell the surplus, as stated in this section from the Council of Cologne in Germany in 1333.

Seeing that our predecessor Henry, of pious memory, ordained by statute that no clerics, secular or monastic, should ply the trade of taverners—yet he would not that this statute should altogether prohibit the selling of such wine as a cleric may derive from his own benefice or from any other source than trade, provided always that this should be done without deceit or fraudulent evasion of the aforesaid statute, and in such manners as have hitherto been used, and decent—yet some men call in question what may be the accustomed and decent manners of sale, to be kept by the clergy in this matter of wine-dealing. We therefore by this present statute have thought good to declare the following as customary and decent fashions of selling wine: to wit, that such sales should be conducted without vociferation or clamour of taverners and (so far as the sellers lieth) without fraud; without tarrying or stay of men drinking such wines either within or at the door of the house, or within the privileged premises wherein such wines are sold; nor, when men would fain drink such wines, may any occasion be given of tarrying or staying at that same place, by the lending of cups or jugs, as is commonly done in taverns of laymen, nor may such be supplied in any way; and these manners aforesaid of selling wine are, in virtue of this present statute, to be used henceforth by clerics.

Quoted in George Gordon Coulton, *Life in the Middle Ages.* Cambridge, UK: Cambridge University Press, 1967, book II.

This detail from an illuminated manuscript shows a monk pouring buckets of wine into a cask.

and bronze. These consisted, not of pigments, but of the actual metals, beaten on an anvil to leaves of a thinness far less than that of the parchment, then delicately pasted on and polished.

Metalwork, Painting, and Architecture

Monastic art was not confined to books. Some monks became metalsmiths, fashioning gold and silver vessels for use at the altar. And, although most of the painters whose works decorated churches throughout the later Middle Ages were professional artists, some were monks, notably Fra Angelico in Italy.

The question of how such lavish decoration was to be reconciled with the plain, simple lives monks and nuns were supposed to lead worried the Cistercian abbot Bernard of Clairvaux, chief proponent of a return to pure Benedictine values. In his *Apologia* condemning the monks of Cluny, he wrote,

> I as a monk ask my fellow monks . . . "Tell me, poor men, if you really are poor what is gold doing in the sanctuary?" . . . vanity of vanities, yet no more vain than insane! The church is resplendent in her walls and wanting in her poor. She dresses her stones in gold and lets her sons go naked. The eyes of the rich are fed at the expense of the indigent [the poor]. The curious find something to amuse them and the needy find nothing to sustain them.[37]

Answering Bernard was Suger, abbot of the great monastery of Saint-Denis near Paris. He argued that the symbol of truth is light, a concept often used by Jesus, and that stained glass windows and gold and silver ornaments reflect such light.

It was Suger who was largely responsible for one of the greatest legacies of monastic art—Gothic architecture. Instead of the dimly lit churches modeled on ancient Roman law courts, or basilicas, Suger envisioned a church where, as he wrote, "the entire sanctuary is thus pervaded by a wonderful and continuous light entering through the most sacred windows."[38]

Suger's view of decoration and architecture prevailed. The dedication of his new church of Saint-Denis in 1144 was attended by every major abbot in France and many from other countries. Awed by what they saw, they hastened to employ in their own churches the innovations he had inspired. As a result, not only the huge abbey churches of Western Europe such as London's Westminster Abbey, but also some of its mightiest cathedrals—Cologne, Reims, York, Notre Dame de Paris—stand as tributes to Suger's vision.

Nuns and monks did not, as did many lay people, separate their work from their practice of Christianity. Instead, they considered work and devotion one and the same, expressions of each other. As the present-day Benedictine nun Norvene Vest writes,

> God's original intention was that work express the unique gifts and

The cathedral of Saint-Denis in France, dedicated in 1144, was the first example of Gothic architecture in Europe.

qualities of each person in the service of a unified whole, like a melody that is diminished by the absence of any single note. Many of us harbor some form of this vision: a deep, often unspoken sense that we have been created for a special purpose, that we have a serious and holy calling to be expressed through active engagement with the world around us—that is, through our work.[39]

Chapter Four

A LIFE OF PRAYER

Work might occupy the hands of medieval monks or nuns, but their minds and hearts had a different focus—worship. This, after all, was the main reason they had sought a monastic life. As the fourth-century monk Evagirus Pontius wrote, "The end [goal] of our profession is the kingdom of God. . . . Everything else, great though it be, must be accounted secondary."[40]

Benedict agreed. While much of his *Rule* dealt with everyday matters, what really mattered most was prayer, both formal and private. This, he wrote, was the monk's *opus dei*, or work of God, to which "let nothing be preferred."[41] In his practical way, however, he sought to define when and how this work would take place.

He seized on two Biblical verses from Psalm 119—"At midnight I rise to praise thee" and "Seven times a day I praise thee for thy righteous ordinances"—and decided that there should be eight offices, or services, each day—one in the middle of the night and seven during the day. This regimen, known as the horarium, or hourly schedule, varied throughout the centuries and from order to order, but in general would survive intact from the time it was first devised by Benedict.

The day of prayer began in the middle of the night, generally about 2 A.M., with Matins. This service is thought to be the most ancient, perhaps dating from the earliest years when Christians were a tiny, persecuted minority meeting in secret under cover of darkness. Matins was both the longest of the offices and the most important, possibly because tradition held that Jesus's resurrection after the crucifixion took place about that time of night.

"Rising Without Delay"

When the bell sounded for Matins, the monks or nuns went directly to the

The Power of Prayer

Medieval monks and nuns believed strongly that prayer had the power to effect change and even to work miracles. St. Bernard of Clairvaux, when a young monk, was not physically strong, but became so because of praying, according to early biographer William of St. Thierry.

At the time of harvest the brothers were occupied, with the fervor and joy of the Holy Spirit, in reaping the grain. Since he [Bernard] was not able to have part in the labor, they bade him sit by them and take his ease. Greatly troubled, he had recourse to prayer and, with much weeping, implored the Lord to grant him the strength to become a reaper. The simplicity of his faith did not deceive him, for that which he asked he obtained. Indeed from that day he prided himself in being more skillful than the others at that task; and he was the more given over to devotion during that labor because he realized that the ability to perform it was a direct gift from God. Refreshed by his employments of this kind, he prayed, read, or meditated continuously. If an opportunity for prayer in solitude offered itself, he seized it; but in any case, whether by himself or with companions, he preserved a solitude in his heart, and thus was everywhere alone. He read gladly, and always with faith and thoughtfulness, the Holy Scriptures, saying that they never seemed to him so clear as when read in the text alone, and he declared his ability to discern their truth and divine virtue much more readily in the source itself than in the commentaries which were derived from it.

William of St. Thierry, "Life of St. Bernard." Quoted in Internet History Sourcebooks Project, Paul Halsall, editor. www.fordham.edu/halsall/source/1150bernard-2accs.html.

church or chapel. In most cases there was no need to get dressed since they slept fully clothed, as Benedict wrote, "that they may be always ready . . . and the sign having been given, rising without delay, let them hasten to outstrip each other to the Work of God, yet with all gravity and decorum."[42]

Heeding their founder's words, the monks would file silently into the chapel. The service began with the chanting or reciting of Psalm 95, the Invitatory, with its familiar opening sentence, "O come, let us sing to the Lord; let us make a joyful noise to the rock of our salvation!"

There was no return to slumber after Matins. Instead the monks or nuns read or prayed privately until time for the next office—Lauds. Lauds, designed to praise God for bringing a new day, was shorter than Matins—about forty-five minutes—and much less somber. Fernand Cabrol, a Benedictine monk and church historian, writes, "The first gleam of dawn recalls to our minds that Christ is the true Light, that He comes to dispel spiritual darkness, and to reign over the world. . . . This tranquil hour, before day has commenced, and man has again plunged into the torrent of cares, is the most favourable to contemplation and prayer."[43] One can well imagine the scene at Benedict's monastery of Monte Cassino in Italy, the black-clad monks lifting their faces to the morning light and repeatedly chanting *laudate dominus*—"praise to the Lord."

Prime, Terce, Sext, None

Throughout much of the Middle Ages, a day officially began with sunrise instead of midnight—1 A.M., for example, would not have been referred to as one in the

Prayer was at the heart of medieval monastic life. This twelfth-century depiction of monks praying was found in a monastery in Egypt.

St. Jerome on Prayer

In his lengthy letter to the nun St. Eustochium, St. Jerome expounded on the exhortation by St. Paul (I Thessalonians 5:17) that Christians should "pray without ceasing."

Although the Apostle [Paul] biddeth us pray without ceasing, and the Saints pray even in their sleep, yet we should have set hours of prayer, in order that time itself may warn us of this duty if by chance we are detained by any work. All know these hours; the third, the sixth, the ninth, daybreak and eventide. Take no food until thou hast prefaced it with prayer; rise not from the table without thanksgiving to thy Creator. In the nighttime rise twice or thrice, and ponder on those Scriptures which thou knowest by heart. Arm thyself with prayer before going forth from thine house; returning from the streets, pray before thou sittest down; let not the body rest until the soul have been fed. At every act, at every step, let thine hand make the sign of the cross.

St. Jerome, "To Eustochium." Internet History Sourcebooks Project, Paul Halsall, editor. www.fordham.edu/halsall/basis/jerome-letter22.html.

morning. So the next office, Prime, came at the end of the first hour of the day, about 6 A.M., followed by Terce, at the third hour (9 A.M.), Sext, at the sixth hour (noon), and None at the ninth hour (3 P.M.). Benedict wrote that when a monk heard the signal for these services, he should, "leaving whatever he hath in his hands, hasten with all speed, yet with gravity, that there may be no cause for levity."[44]

In the early Middle Ages, these services were short—twenty minutes for Prime and ten each for Terce, Sext, and None. The hours were not selected randomly by Benedict, but had great symbolic significance. Terce was the time when the Holy Spirit was said to have descended on Jesus's disciples at Pentecost, the event that marked the actual founding of the Christian church. Sext was midday, when the sun—God's divine light—stood at its highest. None was a more solemn service than the others because it marked the hour when Jesus was said to have died on the cross.

Vespers and Compline

When the day's work was done, the members gathered in the chapel at sunset to celebrate Vespers. It opened with a series of sung or recited psalms, followed by Bible readings. While the object of Lauds was praise, that of Vespers was thanksgiving. Hymns each day of the week expressed thanks for a specific aspect of creation as told in the Book of Genesis. Vespers began anywhere from 4 P.M. to 6 P.M., depending on the time of year, and lasted about a half-hour. In the summer, it was followed by the second meal of the day; in the winter, a light "collation," probably just bread and wine. Then it was time for the day's final office—Compline.

Compline, as its name suggests, completed the day for monks and nuns. Compline was simple and short—psalms, a hymn, a lesson, and a blessing. The services expanded in the later Middle Ages to include a confession of faults thought to have been committed during the day and an absolution, or forgiveness, from the abbot or abbess. After Compline, the monastic community went silently to bed, heeding Benedict's instructions that "there be no more permission from that time on for anyone to say anything."[45]

In the early Middle Ages, then, the monk or nun would spend between three and four hours in communal prayer each day, not counting any Sunday or feast day services. By the time of the height of the Cluny-inspired monasteries about 1000, the eight daily offices had been lengthened by addi-tional readings, hymns, and sermons to the point that they occupied eight hours or more each day. Even Peter Damien, a monk who wanted a return to simpler forms of worship, could not help but be impressed. After one visit to Cluny he wrote its abbot,

When I recall the strict and full daily life of your abbey, I recognise that it is the Holy Spirit that guides you. For you have such a crowded and contin-uous round of offices, such a long time spent in the choir [chapel] serv-ice, that even in the days of midsum-mer, when daylight is longest, there is scarcely half-an-hour to be found, when the brethren can talk together.[46]

Reading Benedict's *Rule*—exactly what psalms were to be read on which day at

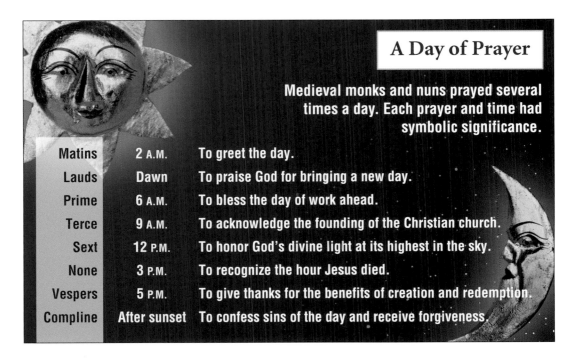

A Day of Prayer

Medieval monks and nuns prayed several times a day. Each prayer and time had symbolic significance.

Matins	2 A.M.	To greet the day.
Lauds	Dawn	To praise God for bringing a new day.
Prime	6 A.M.	To bless the day of work ahead.
Terce	9 A.M.	To acknowledge the founding of the Christian church.
Sext	12 P.M.	To honor God's divine light at its highest in the sky.
None	3 P.M.	To recognize the hour Jesus died.
Vespers	5 P.M.	To give thanks for the benefits of creation and redemption.
Compline	After sunset	To confess sins of the day and receive forgiveness.

St. Augustine's Prayer of Thanksgiving

St. Augustine of Hippo wrote some of the most beautiful prayers in the history of Christianity. This one describes the solace to be found in seeking God in prayer.

Late have I loved Thee, O Lord; and behold,

Thou wast within and I without, and there I sought Thee.

Thou was with me when I was not with Thee.

Thou didst call, and cry, and burst my deafness.

Thou didst gleam, and glow, and dispell my blindness.

Thou didst touch me, and I burned for Thy peace.

For Thyself Thou hast made us,

And restless our hearts until in Thee they find their ease.

Late have I loved Thee, Thou Beauty ever old and ever new.

Thou hast burst my bonds asunder;

Unto Thee will I offer up an offering of praise.

Quoted in "Bibliographical Sketches of Memorable Christians of the Past." http://justus.anglican.org/resources/bio/50.html.

---

what time—might well give the impression that monastic prayer was a by-the-numbers enterprise. Such was not the case. Benedict realized that prayer must be, at its basic level, a personal experience even if done in a communal setting. "If we do not venture to approach men who are in power, except with humility and reverence, when we wish to ask a favor, how much must we beseech the Lord God of all things with all humility and purity of devotion?" he wrote. "And let us be assured that it is not in many words, but in the purity of heart and tears of compunction that we are heard."[47]

Daylong Prayer

Formal services constituted only part of monks' and nuns' lives of prayer. Prayer was to occupy their thoughts during every waking hour, whether they were working or simply sitting quietly. John Cassian, writing in the 300s, reduced constant prayer to a simple formula. He urged his monks to seize on the Bible verse from Psalm 64, "O God, make speed to save me: O Lord, make haste to help me," and then to

let the thought of this verse, I tell you, be conned [repeated] over in your breast without ceasing. Whatever work you are doing, or office you are holding, or journey you are going, do not cease to chant this. When you are going to bed, or eating, and in the last necessities of nature, think on this. . . . Let sleep come upon you still considering this verse. . . . When you wake let it be the first thing to come into your mind, let it anticipate all your waking thoughts, let it when you rise from your bed send you down on your knees, and thence send you forth to all your work and business, and let it follow you about all day long.[48]

In addition, monks and nuns were supposed to translate that prayer into

In this medieval mosaic, a group of monks and well-to-do lay persons pray together during a funeral service.

action, carrying out the will of God. Benedict listed seventy-three types of "good works" ranging from loving God to helping the poor to maintaining silence. These, he wrote, "if they have been applied without ceasing day and night and approved on judgment day, will merit for us from the Lord that reward which He hath promised."[49]

The Object of Prayer

The object of monastic prayers, however, was the same no matter who was offering them or how. Medieval monks and nuns prayed for their own souls, to be sure, and those of their monastic brothers or sisters, but they also prayed for the entire world and even beyond. They prayed for earthly kings, that they might be just and wise rulers. They prayed for the poor and the sick. They prayed for non-Christians throughout the world in the hope that they would be converted.

They also prayed for the dead, specifically those whose souls were in purgatory. Roman Catholic doctrine holds that only the perfect can enter heaven. Those who are not perfect, but whose sins are not serious enough to condemn them to hell, remain in purgatory for a period of time. Devout Catholics believe that prayers can hasten these souls' journey to heaven.

For monks and nuns, prayer was the primary path to knowing God, and that knowledge was their primary purpose in joining their respective orders. As Augustine of Hippo put it,

Let us give your mind's best attention, and, with the Lord's help, seek after God. . . . Let us search for that which needs to be discovered, and into that which has been discovered. He whom we need to discover is concealed, in order to be sought after; and when found, is infinite, in order still to be the object of our search. Hence it is elsewhere said, "Seek his face evermore."[50]

Chapter Five

A LIFE OF LEARNING

When Benedict wrote that he intended "to found a school of the Lord's service,"[51] he did not mean a school in the usual sense. Since some of the people entering the monasteries, both adults and oblates, were illiterate, he considered that the monasteries had a responsibility to make the newcomers literate so they could read and seek to understand the word of God. Consequently, reading—three hours a day or more—was an integral part of the Benedictine's day.

The tools for education are spelled out in the Benedictine *Rule*. Each member was to have a writing tablet and a stylus, or pen. There is specific mention of a library. There was no intent, however, to foster knowledge for its own sake, but as monasticism spread and the *Rule* became the norm throughout Western Europe, monastic schools multiplied and expanded in both who was taught and what was taught. Whether he intended to or not, St. Benedict, as modern Bene-

dictine Hilary Thimmesh writes, "provided for a style of religious life that lent itself to teaching children," so that from 600 to 1100, "it can be said that monastic teachers were the schoolmasters of Europe."[52]

Monastic education had not begun with Benedict. John Cassian, a central figure in spreading monasticism from Egypt into Western Europe in the 300s, founded schools for monks throughout Gaul. When most of continental Europe was overrun by barbarian invasions in the 400s, the focus of education moved to Britain, where Bishop Germanus of Auxerie established several schools.

Cassiodorus

St. Benedict's more immediate successor as an advocate of education was Cassiodorus, a high Roman official who, during the chaos following the barbarian invasions, retired from public life to

become a monk. Possibly following Benedict's example, he founded a monastery, though he did not adopt the Benedictine *Rule*.

Cassiodorus utilized not only classical texts in his monastic educational system, but also the classical view of education. Monks, he believed, should go beyond simple literacy to study what he distinguished as the arts—grammar and rhetoric—and the sciences—arithmetic, music, geometry, and astronomy.

Books copied by Cassiodorus's monks had wide circulation in Italy and Gaul—and beyond. An anonymous scribe wrote that when those areas were overrun by Germanic invaders, "all learned men on this side of the sea took flight,"[53] presumably taking their books with them. The place to which most fled was Ireland.

The Irish had been converted to Christianity in the 400s and had a strongly developed system of monasticism. Indeed, almost the entire religious life of the island was organized around monasteries, instead of bishops as elsewhere. The occupants of these monasteries gladly carried on Cassiodorus's work, copying the Latin classics and bringing decorative illumination to its peak in the process.

St. Bernard lectures a group of monks in a monastery, while a devil tries to tempt a solitary monk in study.

This is not to say that the monks always understood what they were copying. Some who worked in the scriptorium, or writing room, were chosen for their artistic ability rather than their erudition, and sometimes works were copied more for the sake of preservation than study. Moreover, the monks were not necessarily systematic in deciding what to copy. Historian David Knowles notes, "The monks must not be given greater credit than they deserve. They copied what they found to hand; they did little in the way of discovery or presentation. . . . Much of Caesar, Livy and Cicero remained unexploited in solitary bookcupboards."[54]

The Irish Missionaries

Even so, as monastic scholarship declined on the European continent to the point that a French bishop apologized in a written document for his ignorance of grammar, it took firm root in Ireland. The Irish, in turn, would restore that scholarship in the next century as missionaries such as Columba and Columbanus spread learning throughout Europe. They and their disciples founded monasteries, such as Lindisfarne in England, Iona in Scotland, Luxeuil in France, St. Gall in Switzerland, and Bobbio in Italy, that would become famous for their scholarship.

The wave of Irish missionaries continued well into the 800s, when a French monk, Heiric of Auxerre, wrote about "almost the whole of Ireland, despising

A monk is hard at work in a scriptorium in this fifteenth-century manuscript page.

By this point [870], the transmission of European civilization was assured. Wherever they went the Irish brought with them their books, many unseen in Europe for centuries. . . . Wherever they went they brought their love of learning and their skills in bookmaking. In the bays and valleys of their exile, they reestablished literacy and breathed new life into the exhausted literary culture of Europe. And that is how the Irish saved civilization.[56]

Charlemagne's Schools

By the time Heiric was writing, monastic education was on a solid foundation in Europe, thanks not only to missionaries, but also to a king—Charlemagne. Under Charlemagne and the English monk Alcuin of York, monastic education would expand far beyond what it had traditionally been—a vehicle for training future monks. Instead, Charlemagne in 789 decreed that "every monastery and every abbey have its school, in which boys may be taught the Psalms, the system of musical notation, singing, arithmetic and grammar."[57] The decree did not specify which "boys" were to be taught, but a subsequent order by Theodulf, Alcuin's successor as Charlemagne's adviser on education, leaves no doubt. Priests and abbots were ordered to

[ignoring] the sea and its dangers, transporting itself to our shores with a company of its philosophers."[55] They not only reintroduced Christianity in areas where it had fallen into decay, but they also, in author Thomas Cahill's opinion, did much more:

establish schools in every town and village, and if any of the faithful wish to entrust their children to them to learn letters, that they refuse not to accept them but with all charity teach them . . . and let them exact no price from the children for their teaching nor receive anything from them save what parents may offer voluntarily and from affection.[58]

While Charlemagne mentioned only boys in his decree, many schools admitted girls as well, although most were housed in cathedrals rather than monasteries.

Moreover, nuns as well as monks were teachers, at least in the earlier centuries of the Middle Ages. One of the most famous, St. Hilda, was abbess at Whitby in northern England, a "double monastery" housing both monks and nuns.

As a result of Charlemagne's order, two types of monastic schools developed—the *schola claustri* or internal school and the *schola externa* or external school—often within the same abbey. The internal school was for oblates and novices; the external school was for the children

An Encyclopedist's Dilemma

The Dominican friar Vincent of Beauvais was one of the outstanding educators of the Middle Ages. When he was compiling his famous encyclopedia, Speculus Majus, *in the 1200s, he found sources of knowledge at odds with each other. This excerpt from his prologue to the work explains his solution.*

Moreover I am not ignorant that Philosophers have said many contradictory things, especially concerning nature. For example, some have judged the air to be naturally hot, as Aristotle and Avicenna; while others, as Seneca, have pronounced it to be cold. Some also assert that a serpent's venom is frigid, as doth Isidorus; others again will have it to be ardent, of whom is Avicenna. Seeing however that in these and suchlike matters either part of these contradictories may be believed or disbelieved without peril to our Faith, therefore I admonish the reader that he abhor not this book if perchance he find such contradictions in many places, and under the names of divers authors; the more so as I have herein undertaken not the office of a composer but that of a compiler. Wherefore I have taken small pains to reduce the sayings of the Philosophers to concord, striving rather to repeat what each hath said on every matter, and leaving the reader to put faith in one or the other judgment after his own choice.

Quoted in George Gordon Coulton, *Life in the Middle Ages.* Cambridge, UK: Cambridge University Press, 1967, book II.

of those who lived nearby, regardless of social or economic standing.

The Curricular Order

Charlemagne's decree, no doubt influenced by Alcuin, prescribed a specific order in which subjects were to be taught to novices in the *schola claustri*.

First was *psalmos*, learning to read by mastering the Book of Psalms, not only the words themselves, but also their spiritual implications. Next came *notas*, which included penmanship, spelling, and sentence structure. At this point the novices would be qualified to work in the scriptorium copying manuscripts.

King Charlemagne holds audience with his education adviser, Alcuin, who presents the king with a book.

scope than what is taught in today's schools. In external schools, it included some literature, including poetry. In internal schools, it involved the beginning of an in-depth study of sacred works. That study was continued for the most advanced students in the *libros catholicos*, or universal works, which involved studying not only the scriptures, but commentaries on them.

There was rarely a schoolroom in the modern sense. The place most often used was the cloister—a covered walkway, usually forming a square, surrounding a courtyard—that had the advantages of fresh air and light. Students normally sat on the bare stone floor, although in cold weather it might be covered with straw.

Textbooks were rare and costly, so instruction mostly took the form of reading aloud and commentary by the teacher. As the teacher read and commented, students took down what he said on tablets made of thin sheets of wax spread onto wooden forms. Instead of using pens with ink, they wrote in the wax using styluses, pointed sticks made of wood, bone, or—sometimes in the case of noblemen's children—ivory. The writing in wax could be corrected or erased by smoothing it over. More

Their education progressed, however, with the *cantus*, memorizing songs and chants, and then with the *compotus*, using mathematics to explain elements of geometry and astronomy. Astronomy was especially important since the sun, moon, and stars were used to calculate periods of time.

Grammatican came next, but grammar in the Middle Ages was far broader in advanced students learned to write with pens made from goose quills.

With books so hard to come by, monastic pupils had to rely considerably on their own powers of memorization. This was especially true in learning the Psalms, which were recited over and over until they became firmly embedded in the young minds.

Etiquette and Discipline

The head of a monastic or cathedral school went by several titles, but the most common was *scholasticus*. There even seems to have been a sort of vice principal called the *proscholus*. Part of this official's duties, at least as far as the external school was concerned, was to add a dash of etiquette to the curricu-

St. Augustine teaches a class of young students in this Renaissance Dutch painting.

lum. The *proscholus* at the abbey of Fulda in present-day Germany, for instance, instructed his pupils "how to walk, how to bow to strangers, how to behave in the presence of superiors."[59]

The main duty of the *proscholus*, however, was discipline, which doubtless varied in its severity in accordance with the status of the pupil. Oblates and novices could expect more severe punishment, for instance, than the children of a neighboring farmer. They, in turn, would likely not get off as easily as the son or daughter of the local noble.

Corporal punishment was, indeed, considered an integral part of education. Since pupils largely relied on memorization, teachers used various methods to give those memories a boost. The Englishman John of Salisbury, himself a renowned educator, recalled that his grammar teacher had as his goal "to dispense learning according to his pupils' mental capacity. . . . Since memory is improved and talent sharpened by use, he encouraged some by reproofs [rebukes], but others by blows or penalties."[60]

Anselm's View

Not all monastic teachers, however, thought that the best way to impart knowledge to their pupils was to beat it into them. Anselm, abbot of the great French monastery at Bec and later archbishop of Canterbury in England, had more enlightened views. He once compared a colleague's students to a young

A Lack of Learning

In his Ecclesiastes, *a book on historic figures in the church, the priest-philosopher Erasmus told this story to illustrate the sad state of learning among the clergy in the Middle Ages.*

The late bishop of Utrecht, David . . . was a man of conspicuous learning and an excellent theologian, which is very rare among nobles, and especially among bishops of that province, who are burdened with worldly power. He had heard that, among so many who were promoted to Holy Orders, very few were really educated. He resolved to get nearer to the truth, and had his own throne placed in the hall to which the candidates were admitted. He himself propounded questions to each, in proportion to the dignity of the Order which they sought; easier questions to candidates for the subdeaconate, somewhat harder for the deacons, and theological for the priests. Do you ask what happened? He rejected all the candidates but three. Those who usually managed these matters felt that it would be a terrible disgrace to the Church if three only were ordained out of three hundred. The bishop, a man of fervid enthusiasm, answered that it would be a greater disgrace to the Church if they admitted, instead of men, creatures that were more foolish than asses.

Quoted in George Gordon Coulton, *Life in the Middle Ages*. Cambridge. UK: Cambridge University Press, 1967, book II.

Making the Right Impression

St. Anselm, abbot of Bec in France and later archbishop of Canterbury in England, was a firm proponent of education. His view on the impressionability of youth was given by Eadmer, an early biographer.

Anselm's principal concern was for youths and young men, and when asked what the reason for this was, he gave this explanation. He compared the age of youth to wax which is suitably prepared for the impression of a seal. "For if the wax," he said, "is too hard or too soft when stamped with the seal, it will by no means receive the image perfectly. But if it is stamped with the seal at a point between hardness and softness, then the form of the seal will be reflected clearly and completely. Thus it is with the ages of men: . . . Speak with [an elderly] man about spiritual matters, converse with him about the exactness of divine contemplation, show him how to probe heavenly mysteries, and you will observe that he cannot see what you want him to see. No wonder. He is the hardened wax. . . . On the other hand, consider a boy of tender age and little knowledge. . . . Truly the wax is soft and practically liquid and can by no means receive the image of the seal. Midway between these two is the youth and young man suitably tempered in regard to softness and hardness. If you instruct him, you will be able to form him as you wish. Perceiving this, I watch over the young men with greater solicitude, taking care to root out all seeds of vices in them, so that afterwards, when they have been capably instructed in the practice of holy virtues, they may change themselves into the image of a spiritual man.

Eadmer, *Vita Anselmi*. Quoted in St. Anselm College Humanities Program. www.anselm.edu/academic/humanities/eadmer.html.

---

tree around which a fence has been closely built:

They [the students] have been planted in the Garden of the Church by way of Oblation, there to grow and bear fruit to God. But ye so hem them in on every side with terrors, threats, and stripes [whippings], that they can get no liberty whatsoever; wherefore, being thus indiscreetly afflicted, they put forth a tangle of evil thoughts like thorns.[61]

Despite the best efforts of Anselm, Alcuin, Hilda, and a host of other dedicated monks and nuns, monastic education came nowhere near fulfilling the dictates and dreams of Emperor Charlemagne. Monasteries were never numerous enough or close enough to population centers to educate more than a handful of people, and most of those were individuals who intended to join the order.

In addition, the political stability that had allowed monastic schools to flourish did not last. Charlemagne's empire broke up after his death. Fresh waves of invaders—Vikings from Scandinavia, Magyars from Hungary—swept across the land. The monastic schools survived but concentrated on teaching those who would become members. Knowledge of Latin classics declined as church authorities began questioning the use of what they considered "pagan" works. Even Alcuin, in his old age, rejected some of the works and writers he had previously admired.

A Sea of Ignorance

As a result, Western Europe between 900 and 1200 was largely a sea of ignorance in which there were only a few islands of knowledge and learning. Literacy was rare outside the church and almost unknown among the common people, who had only the barest understanding of the basics of their religion. John Bromyard, an English monk in the 1300s, told of asking a shepherd if he knew the Father, Son, and Holy Ghost. "The father and the son I know well, for I tend their sheep," the man answered, "but I know not that third fellow; there is none of that name in our village."[62]

The shepherd could hardly be blamed for his ignorance. While the level of literacy of monks and nuns was fairly high, the same could not be said of ordinary priests. English archbishop John Peckham noted that "the ignorance of the priests precipitates the people into the ditch of [spiritual] error."[63]

But while the monks and nuns of the Middle Ages might not have been able to use the lamp of learning to light up much beyond their own walls, they did keep the lamp lit. And their light, and the knowledge they preserved, would be passed on to the successors of the monastic schools, the universities.

Chapter Six

A LIFE OF VALOR

In 1095 Pope Urban II preached a historic sermon in the French city of Clermont. He called for the Christian kings of Europe to undertake a holy war to recapture Jerusalem, which had been overrun by the Seljuk Turks, and make it once more safe for pilgrims. His listeners responded by shouting "*Deus vult!*" ("God wills it!") and the era of the Crusades had begun. Urban's melding of military and religious zeal would have unforeseen consequences for monasticism. In paving the way for knights to become soldiers of Christ, he also laid the foundation for them to become monks as well—members of the military orders.

The first such order and the most famous was the Knights Templar. After the recovery of Jerusalem by the First Crusade in 1099, the city was open to Christian pilgrims, but the route was more dangerous than ever before. In 1118 a group of nine French knights led by

Guy Hugh de Payens took a vow to defend Jerusalem, although their duties consisted of little more than escorting pilgrims.

King Baldwin II, ruler of Jerusalem, one of four so-called Crusader states established after the First Crusade, gave the group quarters near the site of the ancient Temple of Solomon. First calling themselves the Poor Fellow-Soldiers of Jesus Christ and the Temple of Solomon, they later became known as the Knights of the Temple of Solomon, then the Knights of the Temple, and finally the Knights Templar.

The order remained poor and tiny until 1128, when Hugh returned to France to seek recruits and support. He was highly successful in both but especially in the latter. At a council in Troyes, the Templars' cause was taken up by perhaps the most influential churchman in France, Abbot Bernard of Clairvaux.

Bernard's Essay

It was largely on Bernard's recommendation that the council sanctioned the Templars, and it was he who guided the council in the writing of the order's rule. Furthermore, shortly after the council, Bernard wrote an essay, "On the New Knighthood," that proved highly influential in attracting both recruits and donations of money and property.

In his essay, St. Bernard set forth a justification for acts of violence against non-Christians. Whereas killing another Christian is a homicide, he wrote, killing a pagan was a "mallecide," or a killing of evil. Thus, he wrote,

> The knight of Christ, I say, may strike with confidence and die yet more confidently, for he serves Christ when he strikes, and serves himself when he falls. Neither does he bear the sword in vain, for he is God's minister, for the punishment of evildoers and for the praise of the good.... When he inflicts death it is to Christ's profit, and when he suffers death, it is for his own gain.[64]

The other document that enabled the warrior-monks to reach an eventual state of power and wealth was Omne Datum Optimum, or "All Good Things," a proclamation by Pope Innocent II in 1139. It made the Templars answerable only to the pope, freed them from paying any taxes levied by kings or tithes imposed by bishops, and gave them the right to keep everything captured from their Muslim foes.

Papal protection had also been granted to the Templars' greatest rivals, the Order of St. John of Jerusalem, better

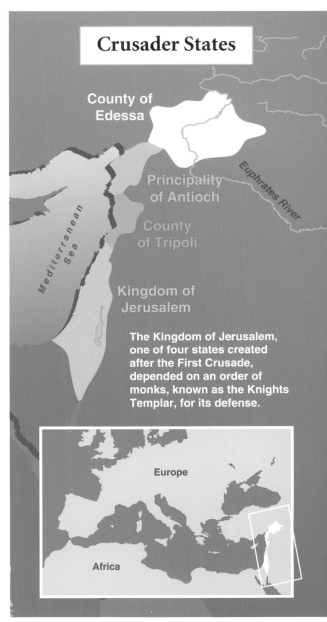

Crusader States

County of Edessa

Principality of Antioch

County of Tripoli

Kingdom of Jerusalem

Mediterranean Sea

Euphrates River

The Kingdom of Jerusalem, one of four states created after the First Crusade, depended on an order of monks, known as the Knights Templar, for its defense.

Europe

Africa

The Templars' Mission

The formal rule of the Knights Templar was given to the order by the Council of Troyes in 1129. The prologue sets forth the purpose and mission of the order.

Above all things, whosoever would be a knight of Christ, choosing such holy orders, you in your profession of faith must unite pure diligence and firm perseverance, which is so worthy and so holy, and is known to be so noble, that if it is preserved untainted for ever, you will deserve to keep company with the martyrs who gave their souls for Jesus Christ. In this religious order has flourished and is revitalised the order of knighthood. This knighthood despised the love of justice that constitutes its duties and did not do what it should, that is defend the poor, widows, orphans and churches, but strove to plunder, despoil and kill. God works well with us and our saviour Jesus Christ; He has sent his friends from the Holy City of Jerusalem to the marches of France and Burgundy, who for our salvation and the spread of the true faith do not cease to offer their souls to God, a welcome sacrifice.

"The Primitive Rule of the Templars," translated by Judith Upton-Ward. The ORB: Online Reference Book for Medieval Studies. www.the-orb.net/encyclop/religion/monastic/t_rule.html.

known as the Hospitallers. This group, far different in origin, dates from 1113 when Pope Paschal II took under his protection Jerusalem's Hospital of St. John and the monastery attached to it.

The Hospitallers

"Hospital" in this case meant both a place for the sick and a hostel, or lodging place, for pilgrims, with the monks attending to their guests' physical as well as spiritual needs. Eventually, those needs included armed escorts, and knights were recruited who, starting in about 1130, took vows similar to those of the Templars.

Also like the Templars, the Hospitallers grew wealthy. The second abbot, Raymond of Provence, found that rich patrons in Europe would rather donate to the military defense of Palestine rather than the care of the sick. As a result, the military function of the order gradually supplanted the original purpose.

Both the Templars and Hospitallers grew far beyond their escort roles, becoming armies—among the finest of the time. They owed their success not to greater skill than other warriors, but to their discipline, spiritual fervor, and disregard for personal safety.

Discipline—following orders from above and maintaining cohesion in battle—was a constant problem for European armies during the Crusades. Knights fought under their own banners and would frequently disregard the battle plan if they saw a chance for personal glory. In addition, command was usually fragmented among rival leaders. The Templars, Hospitallers, and other military monastic orders such as the Teutonic Knights of Germany had no such problems. Obedience was as firmly imbedded in them as in the monks who dwelled in traditional monasteries.

Moreover, these knights fought not for personal fame, wealth, and glory, but only to fulfill their vows of service in the name of Christianity. Likewise, they did not fear death to the extent that their secular counterparts did, for to be killed while fighting for Jesus was considered a privilege. Jacques de Vitry, a theologian preaching to a group of Templars in the 1200s, told them to "believe that every day that dawns is your last."[65]

Unparalleled Bravery

Consequently, the bravery of the military monks was legendary. They utterly refused to retreat, unless ordered to do so by their commanders or outnumbered by more than three to one, and suffered casualties at a much higher rate than other Crusaders. De Vitry wrote that they were always ready "at whatever time of the day or night they may be called, either to fight or to accompany travellers; and when they pursue the enemy, they do not ask, 'How many are they?', but only 'Where are they?'"[66]

As soldiers, the Templars and others had much more in the way of possessions than ordinary monks. Each knight usually had at least two horses—a large destrier, or warhorse, for battle and a smaller horse, known as a palfrey, for ordinary use. He also had armor and was outfitted with the usual weapons of the day—lances, swords, and daggers. The armor and weapons, however, were plain, without decoration, jewels, or gilt.

The warrior monks' robes, though distinctive so as to stand out in battle, were as plain as those of their cloistered

A band of Knights Templar on horseback leads a large army into battle in Palestine.

counterparts. The Templars' rule specified that their robes "must have no superfluity or pride about them, and no brother shall wear any fur, other than a sheepskin . . . and if any brother, through pride or bravado, should covet a better or more beautiful robe, let him be given the vilest of all."[67]

Nothing the knights used or wore, however—horses, clothing, weapons—actually belonged to them. Everything was owned by the order, even the sheepskin undergarments worn by the Templars as a sign of chastity. Their lack of vanity extended to their own bodies as well. The Templars seldom bathed and wore their hair very short (in contrast to the prevailing style).

Neither the Templars nor the Hospitallers had their own priests at first, so they had to depend on local clergy for spiritual support. This arrangement was inadequate when the troops were in the field, so the orders eventually were permitted to have their own priests as members. Rounding out the organization were those who acted as cooks, stewards, and grooms for the horses. These were called farmers by the Templars and serjeants-at-office by the Hospitallers.

Lions and Lambs

The soldier monks presented a sharp contrast in demeanor depending on

A line of Knights Templar leads the defense of Acre in Syria from an attacking Egyptian army in 1291.

where they were and what they were doing. As de Vitry put it, they were "in turn lions of war and lambs at the hearth; rough knights on the battlefield, pious monks in the chapel; formidable to the enemies of Christ, gentleness itself towards His friends."[68]

When not on the march or in battle, the brothers divided their time between monastic and military pursuits. Because of the latter, their daily regimen of prayer was slightly different from those of other orders. The Templars, for instance, rose at either four in the morning or six, depending on whether it was summer or winter. They donned robes over their sheepskin underclothing and went in silence to the chapel, where they recited the prayers for Matins, Prime, Terce, and Sext. Benedict's horarium was not ignored, but elements were combined to free the knights for other duties.

When the prayers were finished, the knights went about various tasks—checking their horses and harness, mending armor, sharpening weapons—before spending the rest of the morning in military exercises. The first meal of the day was at about noon, eaten in silence at long wooden tables while a brother read from the Bible. Although the setting was similar to that of other monastic meals, the food was often different. Because their job included fighting as well as praying, to keep their strength up they ate red meat perhaps three times a week, despite Benedict's disapproval of such fare.

Soon after the midday meal, the members of the order returned to the chapel.

Once more, prayers were combined, in this case None and Vespers. Frequently, however, some monks still had work to do and were permitted to be absent. The Templars made provisions for those who were working. If a brother was in the middle of shoeing a horse when the bell rang for prayers, for instance, he could keep on working, but was required to recite the prayer known as the paternoster, or Lord's Prayer, under his breath the entire time. Prayer, in fact, was almost constant, even when the brothers were engaged in military drills or other work.

The evening meal took place near sundown; then everyone returned to the chapel for Compline, followed by a blessing from the master, as the head of a military order was called, rather than abbot. Everyone then trooped off to bed, sleeping on straw mattresses on the dormitory floor.

Strict Rules

The rules by which the warrior monks lived were, then, just as strict—if not more so as the rules that ordinary monks observed. Perhaps this was because the military brothers generally came from backgrounds much more worldly than those of their more traditional counterparts. The churchmen who drew up the Templar rule, writes historian Piers Paul Read, "seemed more anxious to make monks out of knights than knights out of monks."[69] Those joining the military orders often came from lives of violence, not peaceful contemplation.

Certainly, men joined the military orders for reasons other than seeking their own salvation. The warrior monks' success on the battlefield attracted many recruits. Other recruits were younger sons of noblemen who, since they were not likely to inherit either lands or titles, chose to seek a life elsewhere. Some may have been fleeing debts. One Templar Grand Master, Gérard of Ridefort, was said to have originally joined after being rejected by his lady love.

As the Crusades wore on, the military orders began to lose their focus. For long stretches of time, Palestine was safe from Muslim invasion and pilgrims could come and go in safety. The Templars and Hospitallers then found themselves fighting on behalf of some of the local Christian rulers, almost like mercenaries. They even fought each other at one point in the 1200s when the Hospitallers backed one claimant to the throne in Jerusalem and the Templars backed another.

The reach of the Templars and Hospitallers went far beyond Palestine as they established administrative divisions called commanderies throughout Western Europe. The commanderies served as centers both to solicit gifts and store them. The Templars' commanderies especially gained a reputation as the safest place in the world to store various forms of wealth, since they were well-protected by a well-armed and trustworthy force. Eventually the Templars established what amounted to Europe's first banking system. If a merchant had funds deposited in a Templar stronghold in England, for instance, he could take proof of such holdings with him on a long journey and withdraw money from any other Templar commandery along the way.

The Templars' Undoing

Soon, the Templars began loaning money at interest to nobles, bishops, and even kings—and that proved to be their undoing. Europe's strongest king, Philip IV of France, had borrowed enormous sums from the Templars and saw an opportunity to get rid of both his debt and what he considered an internal threat to his power. He forced the weak Pope Clement V, whose election he had arranged, to approve a secret order to bring all the Templars to trial. In October of 1307, on Friday the thirteenth—a day considered bad luck ever since—Templars throughout Europe were arrested. Under torture, some confessed to dubious charges such as homosexuality and the worship of idols. All their wealth was confiscated, the order was disbanded, and the leaders were burned at the stake.

The Hospitallers fared better. They had not gone into banking or money-lending as had the Templars and thus escaped the Templars' fate. When, in 1291, Muslim armies drove the Crusaders from their last stronghold in the Holy Land, the Hospitallers moved their base of operations successively to the Mediterranean islands of Cyprus and Rhodes. There, they became a naval power, providing transportation for pilgrims to Palestine and battling Muslim pirates. They were

The Templars' Stronghold

The Templars and Hospitallers constructed in Palestine some of the mightiest fortifications the world had seen. The ruins can still be visited. An anonymous knight known as the Templar of Tyre left this description of the Templars' compound in Acre.

At its entrance was a stronghold very high and strong and its walls were very thick, a block of 28 feet (8.5m). On each side of the fortress was a small tower and on each a lion *passant* [seen from one side while walking] as big as a fattened oxen, all covered with gold. The price of the four lions, in material and work, was 1,500 Saracen besants [about $120,000]. It was marvelous to behold. On the other side, toward the Pisan quarter, was a tower. Nearby, above the monastery of the nuns of Saint Anne, was another huge tower with bells and a marvelous and very high church. In addition there was a tower on the beach. This was an ancient tower, a hundred years old, built by command of Saladin [a great Muslim general of the twelfth century]. Here the Templars guarded their treasury. This tower was so near the beach that the sea waves washed it. And many other beautiful abodes were in the Temple, which I will forgo mentioning.

Quoted in Piers Paul Read, *The Templars.* New York: St. Martin's, 1999.

End of the Templars

On October 13, 1307, King Philip IV of France had every member of the Knights Templar in his kingdom arrested and their possessions seized. Shortly afterward, the king's chancellor, William de Nogaret, read Philip's mandate outlining the supposed crimes of the order:

A bitter thing, a lamentable thing, a thing horrible to think of and terrible to hear, a detestable crime, an execrable evil, an abominable act, a repulsive disgrace, a thing almost inhuman, indeed alien to all humanity, has, thanks to the reports of several trustworthy persons, reached our ears, smiting us grievously and causing us to tremble with the utmost horror.*

At first, Pope Clement V was angry at the arrests, writing that Philip had "in our absence, violated every rule and laid hands on the persons and properties of the Templars."** Italy and the Vatican, however, were under the control of French armies at the time, and Clement later had no choice but to agree when the leading Templars were found guilty of heresy and burned at the stake.

* Quoted in Stephen Howarth, *The Knights Templar: Christian Chivalry and the Crusades, 1095–1314.* New York: Atheneum, 1992.
** Quoted in Piers Paul Read, *The Templars.* New York: St. Martin's, 1999.

King Philip IV of France looks on as a group of Knights Templar is burned at the stake.

forced to move their base of operations to Malta in 1530 and only ceased to be a military order in 1798.

The heyday of soldier-monks ended with the Crusades, but other orders were established that rendered services that were other than military. The Franciscans and Dominicans abandoned the restrictions of the monastery and moved out into the world, caring for the poor and sick and preaching the word of God.

Chapter Seven

A LIFE OF SERVICE

The full flowering of monasticism in Western Europe was in the eleventh and twelfth centuries. By 1200 the bloom had begun to fade. Cathedral schools and universities were taking over the monasteries' educational role. While the Cistercians were still faithfully following Benedict's *Rule*, many orders had grown lax. Monasteries amassed great wealth, and monks lived lives of comfort and plenty. The Templars were doing brave deeds in Palestine, but their commanderies in Europe were more about lending money than lending aid.

Renewal was clearly needed, and it came in unexpected forms from unexpected sources—an Italian visionary, a Spanish zealot, and hermits from Palestine forced to reinvent themselves in Europe. Their orders—the Franciscans, Dominicans, and Carmelites—embraced poverty as never before and sent monks outside the monastery walls to serve humankind.

The Franciscans and Dominicans were established at about the same time, 1209 and 1216, respectively, and shared the same mission—taking the word of God to the people. Their founders, however, approached that mission in dramatically different ways.

St. Francis of Assisi, founder of the Franciscans, rejected a life of wealth and leisure in Italy to become an itinerant preacher. He intended this calling to be his alone, with no thought of others joining him, much less of founding a monastic order. His only desire, one of his earliest followers wrote, was "to live according to the holy Gospel."[70]

Francis began preaching wherever and whenever and to whomever he could, even to animals. His sanctity and enthusiasm soon drew followers. He was far too modest to consider these followers disciples. Instead, he said, "the Lord has sent me brothers."[71]

St. Francis and the Animals

St. Francis of Assisi had such a special love for animals that he is their patron saint. He even preached to them. This, for instance, is his famous "Sermon to the Birds," dating from about 1220.

My little sisters, the birds, much bounden are ye unto God, your Creator, and always in every place ought ye to praise Him, for that He hath given you liberty to fly about everywhere, and hath also given you double and triple raiment; moreover He preserved your seed in the ark of Noah, that your race might not perish out of the world; still more are ye beholden to Him for the element of the air which He hath appointed for you; beyond all this, ye sow not, neither do you reap; and God feedeth you, and giveth you the streams and fountains for your drink; the mountains and valleys for your refuge and the high trees whereon to make your nests; and because ye know not how to spin or sow, God clotheth you, you and your children; wherefore your Creator loveth you much, seeing that He hath bestowed on you so many benefits; and therefore, my little sisters, beware of the sin of ingratitude, and study always to give praises unto God.

Quoted in *The History Place Great Speeches Collection.* www.historyplace.com/speeches/saintfran.htm.

St. Francis, the patron saint of animals, preaches to birds in this Italian painting.

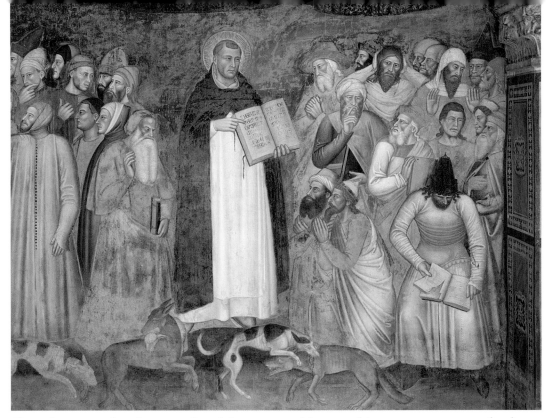

Franciscan monks often wandered the countryside, preaching to common people along the way.

Francis's "Brothers"

The Franciscans—the men, at least—were, indeed, "brothers." The formal name of Francis's initial order was the Ordo Fratrum Minorum, or Order of the Little Brothers. The members were called friars, from the French form of *fratrum*. Francis's group was known as the Friars Minor. Similarly, the Dominicans would be the Ordo Fratrum Praedicatorum, or the Order of Preaching Friars. The orders of friars were called mendicants, from the Latin word for "beggar" since they frequently subsisted only on what people might give them.

Francis decreed, however, that, when possible, his friars should work to earn what they needed, though that did not include money, even money put to good uses. Francis abhorred money to the extent that he hated even to touch it and rebuked some of the friars who did so. It was only later, after the order grew out of all proportion to anything its founder could have imagined, that he relaxed the prohibition.

Francis's little band of friars wandered the countryside singly or in small groups, preaching wherever they could find an audience. More often than not, that audience consisted of common people, country peasants and the poor of towns and cities. That was fine with the Franciscans. They preferred to carry their message to the masses. That message, given in simple, short homilies, emphasized the need for people to prepare themselves for the coming of the kingdom of God.

As the Franciscan movement began, the established church was unsure how to react. Some heretical groups, notably the Albigensians and Waldensians, had sprung up, advocating a return to simple Christianity without pope, cardinals, and bishops. These groups made the church officials understandably nervous. Similarly, ordinary priests resented Franciscan priests preaching, administering communion, and hearing confessions in their parishes.

Papal Blessing

Francis, however, was no heretic. While he would have preferred his brothers not to be ordained, he respected the priesthood and allowed priests to join his order. He also freely acknowledged the authority of the church hierarchy. Given the enthusiasm for religion being rekindled by the Franciscans' efforts, Pope Innocent III therefore gladly granted the order his formal blessing.

The Franciscans actually consisted of three orders. The Friars Minor came first in 1209, followed in 1212 by the Order of Poor Ladies, also known as the Poor Clares. This group had its beginning when Clare of Assisi, the daughter of a noble family, heard Francis preach and immediately decided to dedicate her life to God. A few nights later she left her family's house in secret to meet Francis

and a few of his followers. She cut off her hair, dressed in a coarse robe with a thick veil, and took a vow of poverty.

Franciscan sisters could not wander the countryside in safety, so Clare was eventually housed beside a chapel Francis had rebuilt. She was soon joined by other women similarly taken with his message. The sisters did not go forth to preach or work among the poor, but rather remained behind the convent walls, leading lives of prayer and contemplation, supporting themselves through donations and by selling bread they baked or religious items they crafted.

The remaining order, the Brothers and Sisters of Penance, was a testimony to Francis's genius. He recognized that some people, though restricted by marriage or other family ties, could still contribute much to God's work. Members of the Third Order, as it is still generally known, lived as ordinary citizens, but under a modified Franciscan rule. They were to dress simply, fast and pray often, refrain from violence, and work to relieve the suffering of the sick and poor.

Wherever they went, in their daily activities the Franciscans stressed making a connection to common people and their everyday concerns. Their message was based on the emotional appeal of Jesus's parables, and their success was partially due to the sprit of the times. The middle classes, especially in Italy, were gaining a sense of their potential. They welcomed the Franciscans' message of simple Christian living, which was to have a lasting and perhaps unintended effect. Modern historian Norman Cantor writes, "Franciscan puritanism and naturalism sanctified and nourished the sentiments of the common man—a crucial precondition to democracy and mass culture."[72]

The Dominicans

Far different was the preaching of the Dominicans, founded by the Spanish scholar Dominic Guzman. The purpose of the order, as laid down by Dominic in the order's *Constitutions*, was "preaching and for the salvation of souls."[73] Specifically, the Dominicans' goal was to refute heresy. As such, the members needed to be erudite, intellectual, and solidly grounded in theology. For that reason, the Dominicans placed great emphasis on education. Prospective members had to be literate and had to complete rigorous schooling before they were sent out to preach.

The Dominican friars also had to be priests, another difference from the Franciscans. Dominic believed that laxity among the clergy had caused heresies to arise and that ordained priests should be employed to battle them. However, like Francis, he demanded that his followers take a vow of poverty, have no personal property or income, and make their way by begging.

Intellectual Contributions

When Dominicans were training to become preachers, or when preachers

Clare of Assisi dedicated her life to God after she heard Francis preach.

returned for a time to the monasteries, education was their chief occupation. Unlike other monastic orders, they were not assigned any manual labor. The operation of the monastery was left entirely in the hands of lay brothers. This is not to say that the preachers considered themselves in any way superior. The

The works of Thomas Aquinas were eventually adopted as the official doctrine of the Roman Catholic Church.

Pope Honorius III made Dominic Master of the Sacred Palace. This office, in essence the pope's chief theologian, would be held by a Dominican even into the twenty-first century.

The Dominicans were major contributors to the intellectual life of Europe. Many of their recruits came from university towns, and many Dominicans eventually became leading faculty members at their local universities. They shaped theological life and teaching at Oxford and held virtually all the most important posts at the University of Paris.

The rise of the Dominicans coincided with the reintroduction into Europe of the writings of Greek philosophers. Among them were the works of Aristotle, and it became the challenge of the Dominican intellectuals to reconcile his philosophy of rationalism with Christianity. The Dominicans were equal to the challenge, providing some of the greatest minds and innovative thinkers of the Middle Ages. Chief among them was Thomas Aquinas, who in his *Summa Theologica* presented a carefully constructed theological model defending Christian principles. His works were later adopted as the official doctrine of the Roman Catholic Church.

preachers and lay brothers slept in the same dormitories and ate in the same refectories. The lay brothers were served their meals first, in fact, and the prior, or head of the monastery, last.

The Dominicans were, in Cantor's words, "the intellectual shock troops of the thirteenth-century church."[74] Their standing and reputation was such that in 1218

Because of the rigorous standards for membership, the Dominicans were never as numerous as the Franciscans, who by 1250 had grown to more than thirty thousand members. At their height in the mid-1300s, there were about twelve thousand preachers and seven thousand lay brothers. Their impact on society, however, was out of all proportion to their numbers. Not only in theology, but also in politics, as advisers to kings, and in art, producing such Renaissance masters as Fra Angelico and Fra Bartolommeo, the Dominicans left their mark on civilization.

The Carmelites

Although the Franciscans and Dominicans were the most numerous and influential of the friars, there were two other mendicant orders in the Middle Ages, the Carmelites and the Augustinians, that contributed to the intellectual growth and spiritual well-being of Europe. The basic mission of the Carmelite friars was to teach. They did so at all levels, from local schools to universities. They were not as constantly on the move as the Franciscans and Dominicans, many enjoying the stability of being assigned to a single monastery. They were also, however, in the forefront of missionary work, sending

Tales of St. Dominic

In 1259, almost thirty years after St. Dominic's death, one of his followers, Gerard de Frachet, wrote down collected stories about him. Many deal with miracles he is supposed to have performed, but two give insights into his character.

So wonderfully tender-hearted was he touching the sins and miseries of men, that when he came near any city or town from where he could overlook it, he would burst into tears at the thought of the miseries of mankind, of the sins committed therein, and of the numbers who were going down into hell. If it chanced that after the fatigues of a long journey he had to lodge with secular persons, he would first quench his thirst at some handy spring, fearing to draw attention to any

excess in drinking from his intense thirst, due to his wearisome traveling on foot. This he was always most careful to avoid, not only in drinking, but in everything else besides. . . . His heart was so centred in God that in the things of this world he kept himself detached not only from everything that was in any sense of the word precious, but even from things that were poor or of less consequence, as was apparent in his books, his clothes, belt, shoes, knife (a thing he seldom carried), and the like, which were all of the poorer sort, shunning everything that was either becoming or curious.

Quoted in *Lives of the Brethren of the Orders of Preachers, 1206–1259*. www.op.org/domcentral/trad/brethren/breth 02.htm.

brothers to the west coast of Africa, to Asia, and eventually to the Americas to teach and win converts for Christianity. One history of the order tells that "whenever there was a spiritual need, the Carmelites reached out in a unique fashion as contemplatives in action."[75]

While women's orders developed parallel to men's among the Franciscans and Dominicans, it was not until the mid-1400s that the first Carmelite sisters came into being. They expanded quickly, however, especially due to the reforms initiated in 1562 by the Spanish nun Teresa of Ávila. With the help of the Spanish monk who called himself John of the Cross, she founded nunneries and friaries

that eventually became part of the Carmelite order. These groups returned to a less intellectual and more secluded way of life.

The Augustinians

Like the Dominicans and Carmelites, the Augustinians were scholars and teachers. They were active in universities and also established their own schools. While they produced numerous theologians, they also tended toward the study of natural sciences.

The Augustinians, however, were known for sanctity as well as dedication to science. A disproportionate

A procession of Carmelite nuns exits their church as other nuns tend to the convent's gardens.

number became the confidants and confessors to kings, bishops, and even popes. Ever since the late 1200s, an Augustinian friar has been the official sacristan to the pope, charged with always being near the pontiff, ready to administer communion in case of serious illness.

The Augustinians, like the other mendicant orders, had a companion order of nuns. There was a major difference, however, in that the Augustinian sisters very early—in 1401—began accepting lay members. These women took vows that permitted them to work outside the convent in schools and hospitals.

The attitude of the people of the later Middle Ages toward traditional monks and nuns was divided. They were respected for their sanctity and at the same time considered a drain on society because their orders grew rich while they themselves seemed to do little or no work. The mendicant friars did much to change that ambiguity. While maintaining the ancient devotion to prayer, they also put the spirit of monasticism to work, perhaps ensuring that the spirit would continue in future centuries.

Chapter Eight

A Life Unchanging

Early in its history, the Christian church began a slow, yet pronounced, division into Eastern and Western branches centered respectively in Constantinople and Rome. Although the climactic breach—still unhealed—would not occur until 1054, the two branches of the church developed in different ways in matters of practice as well as of basic doctrine.

Thus, while Christianity in Western Europe was marked by constant reform and renewal, in the East it lived, as historian Brian Moynahan writes, "off its inheritance. Its purpose was *agalma*, or 'statuesque calm,' and it lacked the restless dynamic that stamped the Western faith."[76] As a result, Eastern—eventually known as Orthodox—monasticism, although it developed early in different ways from its Western counterpart, remained essentially the same throughout the Middle Ages, and, indeed, to the present day.

One reason for this stability was that the principles of Eastern monasticism were almost entirely derived from a single source—Basil the Great—whereas there were various rules in the West, although St. Benedict's became the norm. St. Basil's rules, known as the *Asceticon*, formed the foundation for all Eastern monasticism.

The other source of stability was the strong central government headquartered in Constantinople. In the East the emperor held sway over both secular and religious matters. From time to time church leaders convened in councils and the resulting edicts issued by emperors were binding on monasteries throughout the Eastern Roman Empire.

The *Asceticon*

Basil, born in 329, decided early in his monastic career that community life was superior to that of hermits. He set forth several reasons for his decision. How could one discover his faults, he asked, if there was no one to correct him? How can one be patient in the absence of any demands? How can one be charitable when there is no one to give to?

Basil knew, however, that people living together needed some kind of code of conduct. Thus, he wrote the *Asceticon* for monks and nuns in the many houses he helped establish. It was not a rule in the Benedictine sense, prescribing every detail of the monk's or nun's life down to which psalms should be sung on which days. Instead, it was a set of principles constructed around four major themes— poverty, obedience, renunciation of one's former life, and renunciation of one's self.

The *Asceticon* was set down in two parts, the Greater Rules and Lesser Rules, sometime called the Greater and

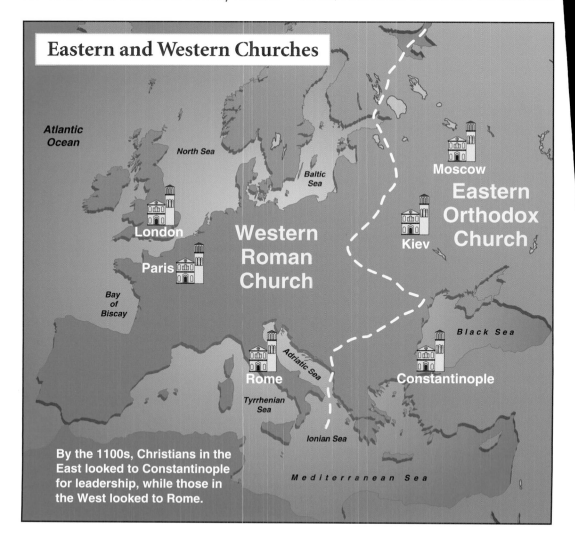

Eastern and Western Churches

Atlantic Ocean

North Sea

Baltic Sea

Moscow

Eastern Orthodox Church

London

Western Roman Church

Kiev

Paris

Bay of Biscay

Black Sea

Rome

Adriatic Sea

Constantinople

Tyrrhenian Sea

Ionian Sea

By the 1100s, Christians in the East looked to Constantinople for leadership, while those in the West looked to Rome.

Mediterranean Sea

Questions because Basil used as [a] format a series of questions and [answers] between a pupil and master. The [answers] gave practical examples and [in]cluded a verse from the Bible to [drive] the point.

[For] instance, Question 30 of the Greater [Rules] asks, "In what spirit should superi-[ors w]ork for brothers?" The answer is:

[T]he superior should not be made [p]roud by his dignity, lest he miss out [o]n the blessing promised to the hum-[b]le or be blinded by pride and fall under the judgment given to the devil. He should be convinced that to gov-ern is to serve. Take the case of some-one who cares for an injured man. He cleans the pus from his wounds and uses remedies appropriate to the evil he faces. He does not become at all vain because of the service he is giv-ing. Rather he finds in it a source of humility, concern and anguish. In the same way and even more so, the one who has the charge of curing the com-munity, as one who serves everyone and is bound to respond to each one, has to accept worries and anxiety. Then he will really reach his goal, according to the word of the Lord: "He who would be first among you must be last of all and make himself the servant of all" (Mark 9:34).[77]

Moral Guideposts

Basil's fifty-five Greater Rules and 315 Lesser Rules are moral guideposts rather than dictates. It was left to subsequent councils to fill in the blanks. Consequent-ly, Eastern monasteries never composed a monastic order in the Western sense. Instead, monasteries were largely inde-pendent of one another. Historian Jules Pargoire writes, "It is not enough, to affirm that the Basilian Order is a myth. One must go farther and give up calling

Basil dictates his Asceticon *to a team of scribes.*

the Byzantine [Orthodox] monks Basilians. Those most concerned have never taken this title, and no Eastern writer that I know of has ever bestowed it upon them."[78]

The *Asceticon* and subsequent edicts did, however, produce a way of life that extended throughout the Eastern Empire. Most aspects of a monastery came to be known by Greek names. The monastery itself was called the *laura*, and its leader was the *hegoumenos*, who was elected by the membership on the basis of merit. Then, in a major departure from Western practice, the new *hegoumenos* received his staff of office from the emperor.

Another difference from Western monasticism was that the *hegoumenos* was almost always a priest, and it was he who most administered to his flock's spiritual needs. Under the *hegoumenos* were a host of other offices, mostly of the same kind as in the West, but with different titles. The prior was the *deutereuon*, the sacrist was the *hepistemonarchos*, and so forth.

Double Monasteries

Basil's initial foundation and many of those that followed were double monasteries that included a nunnery, an arrangement rarer in the West but not unknown. Contact between the sexes was allowed in very limited, strictly supervised circumstances. In later centuries women's houses came to be built separately and were more strictly enclosed than were the men's houses, just as in the West.

Spirit Willing; Flesh Weak

St. Basil the Great was a great traveler and enjoyed visiting not only the monasteries he helped establish, but also his fellow church leaders. Late in life, however, his health would not permit him to travel in the winter, as this letter to a physician named Melitius shows.

I don't suppose that the cranes are better than I am at predicting the future, but I cannot fly and am not as free as a bird in my choice of life either, so unlike the cranes I am not able to get away from the hardships of winter. For one thing there are some responsibilities in my life that I cannot escape. But besides that, violent fevers hit me without pause—no one thinner than I was had ever been seen, but now there is one, and it is I myself—then came more than twenty rounds of quartan fever, so that now, even with the fevers apparently ended, I am as weak as a spider's web. The result is that I just have to hide out in my room until spring comes, if I can last that long without succumbing to the intestinal disorder now under way. But if the mighty hand of the Lord upholds me, I will be glad to come to your land to have the chance to embrace you, dear friend. But pray that my life may be ordered to the advantage of my soul.

St. Basil the Great, "To Melitius, the Noted Physician." Quoted in *The Life of St. Basil*. www.basilian.org/Publica/StBasil/Stbasil4.htm.

This illuminated manuscript page depicts a scene in the life of a nun, as she takes confession and prays privately.

The earliest monasteries accepted newcomers as full brothers or sisters, but a system soon began whereby applicants entered as postulants and after a probationary period of six months became novices. The practice of giving children as oblates was not unknown, and children as young as ten could make their initial vows. Married men could join, providing their wives agreed to release them from their marriage vows. Male postulants were received as novices in a ceremony in which their hair was cut into a tonsure shaped like a cross and they received a tunic and a tall cap known as the *kalimauchoin.*

Basil placed a great deal of value on work, and novices had to prove themselves not just spiritually, but with hard labor. Once the novice became a monk he was expected to pursue a trade as assigned by the superior, using tools owned by the community. Although the monasteries were autonomous, there was much cooperation among them, and some specialized in either manufactured goods or foodstuffs that might be traded.

After three years, novices became full members in a ceremony called the *mystegion monachikes teleioseos,* or sacrament of monastic perfection, in which they swore to renounce their former lives and to obey the rules of the laura. The monks received a new tunic, along with a special cloak called the *mandyas,* or angelic habit, also called the lesser habit. The new member recited a special prayer, received communion, and from that time onward was bound to the monastery.

Even this, however, did not complete the process of becoming a monk. A custom arose that, after a few years of service, a monk might receive a larger cloak called the greater habit. This called for another ceremony and tended to create a caste system within the monastery, to the dismay of some leaders. St. Theodore of Studium was one who objected, writing, "As there is only one baptism, so there is only one habit."[79]

Life in an Eastern Monastery

The daily life of monks and nuns was much the same as in the West—a combination of prayer and work. It was different, however, in that Eastern monasteries tended to be in or around cities rather than deliberately situated in remote areas. Accordingly, sisters and brothers became much more a part of their communities much earlier. Many houses had orphanages and hospitals attached, and some members were assigned to study medicine.

Otherwise, monks and nuns were expected to live simply, quietly, and soberly. Food was plain, usually what could be grown or obtained locally. The daily meal consisted of fruit and vegetables. On feast days fish and dairy products might be added. Guests dined on the same fare served to the members.

Novices were instructed to maintain silence except in prayers and when spoken to by the novice master or another superior. Otherwise, members were to speak only briefly and out of necessity,

Eulogy for St. Basil

The most important figure in the history of Eastern monasticism was St. Basil the Great, whose Asceticon *remains the basic guidepost for Orthodox monks and nuns. In 381, two years after Basil's death, a eulogy was delivered by his brother, Gregory of Nyssa, who ended by saying:*

Brethren, having imitated his discretion by appropriating it, let us praise virtue according to [Basil's] worthiness and fulfill all his wonderful deeds by sharing his wisdom. By praising poverty we become poor with regard to material wealth. . . . [Basil] stored up his own wealth in the treasure house of heaven, so imitate the teacher in this way. The disciple will be perfect when he resembles the master. In other occupations one is a disciple to a physician [or] geometrician, and a person studying rhetoric will be not be worthy of his master's art unless he admires this skill by speech, for he has not yet shown himself worthy of such respect. Allow someone to say to him, "How can you say that a physician is a master when he has no knowledge of his skill? How [can] you say one is a geometrician when he has no knowledge of his craft?" But if anyone demonstrates expertise in what he has learned, his own knowledge will honor his master's instruction. Thus we who magnify the teacher Basil should reveal his teaching by our lives because his name honored God and men in Christ Jesus our Lord, to whom be glory and power forever and ever.

Gregory of Nyssa, "A Eulogy for Basil the Great." Quoted in Black Hills State University College of Arts and Sciences. www.bhsu.edu/artssciences/asfaculty/dsalomon/nyssa/basil.html.

and laughter was forbidden. Although they vowed to renounce their former lives and changed their names on taking vows, the Eastern monks and nuns were allowed to retain familial ties to a greater extent than many of their Western counterparts. They could write to relatives and receive occasional visits. There were even provisions for the monastery to take in and care for members' relatives who found themselves in dire poverty.

Eastern Mysticism

Despite such practicalities, Eastern monasticism was mystical to a far greater extent than in the West, reflecting other religious practices in the area such as Zoroastrianism in Persia and the Egyptian worship of Isis and Osiris. Although Basil's *Asceticon* showed a marked preference for communities, there remained an appreciation for the hermit's way of life. If a monk decided to follow such a calling, he could do so, but could return any time he wished.

The monks withdrew, as had St. Anthony in Egypt two centuries earlier, to seek God, not only through solitude, but through "mortifying the flesh"— undergoing pain and suffering in an effort to bring spiritual insight. No person more greatly personifies the Eastern hermit-mystic than St. Simeon, who was known as the Stylite (from *stulos*, the Greek word for pillar). Simeon joined a monastery in Syria at the age of sixteen, but found life there too easy. He first spent three years in a small hut in the desert, but then decided that exposure to the elements might bring him closer to God. Simeon then found a rocky hill, where he bound himself using a chain only ten feet long.

Pilgrims sought out Simeon, asking him to teach and bless them. They eventually took up so much of his time that he decided to place himself atop a pillar in order to avoid them. His first pillar was nine feet high, not sufficient to allow him to escape the voices from below. Gradually, he placed himself higher and higher, finally reaching a perch sixty feet above the ground. There, he spent the last twenty years of his life.

There were other practices peculiar to the area. By the 800s some monasteries were straying from Basil's ideal. Prayers and chanting were getting more complex, and work was being left to lay brothers, as in the West. Theodore of Studium (a monastery near Constantinople) instituted a series of reforms that largely brought monastic life back to its traditional form.

St. Simeon spent the last twenty years of his life in complete seclusion atop a sixty-foot pillar.

Separation of the Sexes

One of Theodore's reforms was the strict separation of monks from nuns. Indeed, Theodore seems to have had a great aversion to women and wanted monks to avoid them as much as possible. In a letter to a fellow abbot, he wrote, "Do not make friends with any canoness, nor enter any women's monastery, nor have any private conversation with a nun, or with a secular woman, except in case of necessity; and then let it be so that two are present on either side. For one, as they say, is cause of offense."[80]

Under Theodore's influence, some monasteries attempted to shut themselves off altogether from contact with women. The most extreme case was—and still is—the monastic community at Mount Athos, a mountainous peninsula extending from northern Greece into the Aegean Sea. In the 900s it became home to twenty monasteries and dozens of hermit's dwellings. Some were perched on rocky crags unreachable even on foot, and both people and supplies had to be pulled up in baskets.

While it was extremely unlikely that any outsider—man or woman—would

Emperor Constantine Monomachos founded Nea Moni and other highly secluded monasteries in an attempt to limit the monks' contact with women.

On Being a Superior

St. Theodore of Studium was one of the most influential figures in Eastern monasticism. When near death in 826, he dictated a final testament to his disciple and designated successor, Naukratios, containing these words of advice.

But now, my father and brother, whoever you are, before God and his chosen angels I entrust all the community in Christ to you so that you may receive it. But, how should you accept? In what grand manner should you guide them? In what fashion should you guard them? As the lambs of Christ! As your own dear limbs! Cherish and respect them, loving each one of them with an equal measure of charity since each man cherishes the limbs of his body equally. Open your heart in sympathy, welcome them all in mercy. Nurse them, reform them, make them perfect in the Lord. Sharpen your understanding with prudence; rouse your will with courage; make your heart steadfast in faith and hope. Lead them forward in every good work. Defend them against spiritual enemies. Shield them, regulate them. Introduce them to the place of virtue. Distribute shares in the land of tranquility.

St. Theodore of Studium, *Testament*. Quoted in "Byzantine Monastic Foundation Documents," Dumbarton Oaks Research Library and Collection. http://www.doaks.org/typikapdf/typ009.pdf.

want to visit such a place, Emperor Constantine Monomachos enacted a law in 1046 that prohibited not only women, but female animals of any kind from setting foot on Mount Athos. Consequently, over the last millennium, there have been rams but no ewes, roosters but no hens, bulls but no cows. The only exception—impossible to regulate—are the wild birds that nest along the cliffs.

It was a peculiarity of the Eastern church that priests were allowed to marry, but monks and nuns had to remain celibate. Since celibacy was also required of bishops, these leaders tended to be drawn from the ranks of the monks. This had the effect of embroiling the monasteries in religious controversies—not polite theological debates, but raging arguments that involved ordinary citizens as well. Monks occasionally were organized into what today would be called pressure groups. As historian David Knowles writes, "Questions such as the morality of an emperor's marriage or remarriage, and deeper issues such as the veneration of images, were debated and sometimes even decided by the monks of the capital [Constantinople], while at certain epochs they had a name [reputation] for rioting and violent action."[81]

An Era of Decline

Such monastic activism and, indeed, the entire scope of Christian influence on governmental and religious affairs would come to an end in the mid-1400s. Starting in the 600s, the forces of Islam began their great period of conquest. One by one, the centers of Eastern Christianity—Jerusalem, Alexandria, Damascus—were taken over. When, in 1453, the Muslim Ottoman Turks took Constantinople, the conquest was complete. Christianity became a minority religion, and monks and nuns gradually adopted a life in the tradition of Evagrius of Pontus, who preached what he called *apatheia*, a diminution of passions and a seeking of harmony. Eastern monasteries were content to reach such harmony and remain small Christian islands in a sea of Islam, and the character of Eastern monasticism has changed little since.

It was at about the same time that cataclysmic changes would also affect monasticism in the West. The once indivisible body of the Roman Catholic church would be ripped apart by the Protestant Reformation. The Middle Ages would give way to the Renaissance, and monasticism would undergo radical and permanent changes.

Epilogue

TWILIGHT
AND LEGACY

Despite the good works and renewal efforts by the Franciscans, Dominicans, and other mendicant monks and nuns, monasticism was at a low ebb in Europe in the 1400s. Sparked by the Renaissance's rebirth of classical learning, people began questioning basic religious doctrines in ways previously unthinkable. The spiritual began to give way to the rational. Monasteries and convents once viewed as the heart and soul of their communities began to be seen as centers of greed and corruption.

While some of the criticisms might have been valid, the real truth was that the world had changed and monasticism had not changed with it. It was an inherently insular, inward-looking institution that failed to adapt to the new ways in which people viewed themselves and the world around them. Consequently, European monasticism, as David Knowles writes, "spiritually weak as it was . . . was

in no good case to weather the unexpected storm of the Reformation."[82] And yet, although it would be all but extinguished in many areas and much diminished in others, monasticism left a rich legacy without which modern civilization would be much poorer.

A foreshadowing of the storm was evident in the writings of English reformer John Wycliffe. In the 1370s, he attacked the wealth of the church, saying it should return to its roots of poverty, preaching, teaching, and service. He was especially critical of monasteries, not only because of their wealth, but because, he said, there was no justification for them in the Bible. Wycliffe's work and views were later taken up by others, including Jan Hus and Martin Luther.

Luther, the man generally credited with beginning the Reformation, was especially harsh in his criticism, although he himself was an Augustinian monk. In 1523 he wrote, of preaching and *Seelsorge* [pastoral care] to them than it would be to have Mohammedans or Jews. These men should only drive asses and lead dogs.[83]

The Popular View

The general opinion of monks and nuns was reflected in the popular literature of the time. In his *Canterbury Tales*, Geoffrey Chaucer held monks and nuns up to ridicule. And Chaucer's friend and contemporary, John Gower, wrote,

[Monks] avoid being hungry and slake their thirst with wine. . . . Faintness of the belly does not come upon them in the hours of night, and their raucous voice does not sing the heights of heaven in chorus with a drinking cup. . . . And while you are bringing him wine, he allures women to himself; wanton monasteries now furnish these two things together.[84]

Church reformer Martin Luther adopted an extremely harsh view of monastic life in his writings.

Our bishops, abbots, and other leaders . . . sit in the devil's place and are become wolves, who neither wish to teach the Gospel, nor to suffer it to exist. So it is no more appropriate to turn over the office

When the Reformation came, it spread quickly across northern Europe, eliminating centuries of Roman Catholic tradition, including monasticism. In the northern German states, England, and Switzerland, monastic institutions virtually disappeared. In some cases, this process was slow; in others, quick and violent. During the Thirty Years' War in Germany, many abbeys and convents were looted and burned along with other Roman Catholic structures. In England, King Henry VIII legislated the monasteries out of existence, largely to enrich himself by selling off their properties that he had seized.

But while monasticism was severely weakened, it was by no means dealt a fatal blow. Roman Catholic leaders, forced to face the merits of some of the criticism mounted against them, convened a great council at Trent in northern Italy. The council issued several reforms, and it was this reformed version of monasticism that not only survived, but strengthened in such countries as Italy and Spain. The Catholic Church even went on the offensive thanks to a new type of order, the Society of Jesus, or Jesuits. Founded by a former soldier named Ignatius of Loyola, the Jesuits set up schools and colleges for the training of both priests and laymen, but they also went secretly, and in great danger, into Protestant countries to minister to faithful Catholics.

Contributions

However, monks and nuns never regained the place they had occupied during the Middle Ages. Their golden age was past, but the contributions they had made would endure to the present. "They not only established the schools, and were the schoolmasters in them, but also laid the foundations for the universities," writes historian Alexander Flick. "They were

the thinkers and philosophers of the day and shaped the political and religious thought. To them, both collectively and individually, was due the continuity of thought and civilization of the ancient world with the later Middle Ages and with the modern period."[85]

In 1534 Ignatius of Loyola founded the Society of Jesus, a Catholic order whose chief aim was to combat the spread of Protestantism.

In this sixteenth-century Dutch painting, St. Augustine sends his monks out into the world to found new monastic communities and to spread the word of God.

Many of these contributions were far removed from spirituality, but had everything to do with practicality. Much that was innovative in agriculture came about because of careful observation and patient experimentation by monks. They introduced new crops and methods of planting, bred new strains of livestock, and thereby helped to enable the population of Europe to grow.

The monks were technological innovators, as well. They harnessed wind and water for purposes as varied as irrigation and keeping track of time. They were miners and metallurgists whose techniques spread throughout the Christian world.

The brothers and sisters both preserved and passed on learning. Through the copying of Latin classics they forged the link that maintained a connection from the thinkers of the past to those of the present. And their monastery and convent schools were, for centuries, the only place in Western Europe where any learning took place. If the great universities were pinnacles of learning in the Middle Ages, the humble convent school was the foundation.

Almost as important as the preservation of learning was the way in which it was done. The illuminated manuscripts of the fourth and fifth centuries remain among the finest expression of humankind's search for beauty. This search would also find monastic expression in the exquisite needlework of English nuns, the soaring cathedrals taking shape from the vision of French abbots, and the transformation of faith to canvas of Italian monks.

Servants of God

The nuns and monks of the Middle Ages, however, did not consider themselves farmers, teachers, or artists. They were, first, instruments and servants of God, and it is in this area that their greatest achievements lie.

When monasticism began in the deserts of Egypt, Christianity was not the powerful force it is today, but one small faith struggling against many others. It was the monks and nuns who perhaps most clearly heeded the message of that faith's founder, Jesus of Nazareth. Not only did they carry that message throughout the medieval world, but they also became living examples of what Jesus preached.

Thus, throughout centuries often dark and brutal, the monks and nuns held aloft the lights of piety, charity, humility, and kindness. They hold them still. David Knowles writes that monasticism "will remain as a Christian way of life for a greater or smaller number of individuals, with a significance greater than its numerical strength, and if a particular generation (even though it be our own) destroys it or disfigures it, it will return again . . . to show its nobility to the modern world."[86]

Notes

Introduction: The Rise of the Monastic Movement

1. David Knowles, *Christian Monasticism.* New York: McGraw-Hill, 1969, p. 25.

Chapter One: The Search for the Soul

2. St. Augustine of Hippo, *Confessions,* translated by Albert C. Outler. Internet History Sourcebooks Project, Paul Halsall, editor. www.fordham.edu/halsall/basis/confessions-bod.html.
3. St. Augustine, *Confessions.*
4. Quoted in *The Benedictine Oblate Newsletter,* no. 00/4, December 2000–February 2001. St. Gregory's Chapter, Holy Trinity Abbey, New Norcia, WA. www.newnorcia.wa.edu.au/oblate_dec_feb_2001.htm.
5. John Eudes Bamberger, "If Anyone Is in Christ, He Is a New Creature. The Old Has Passed Away; Look! Everything Is New." Abbey of the Genesee. www.abbotjohneudes.org/c12aug01.html.
6. St. Benedict of Nursia, *The Holy Rule of St. Benedict,* translated by Boniface Verheyen. Christian Classics Ethereal Library. www.ccel.org/b/benedict/rule2/rule.html.
7. St. Augustine of Hippo, "On the Work of Monks." *Catholic Encyclopedia.* www.newadvent.org/fathers/1314.htm.
8. "What Is Benedictine Spirituality?" *St. Vincent Archabbey.* http://benedictine.stvincent.edu/archabbey/vocations/vows.html.
9. Athanasius of Alexandria, *Life of St. Antony,* translated by H. Ellershaw. Internet History Sourcebooks Project, Paul Halsall, editor. www.fordham.edu/halsall/basis/vita-antony.html.
10. St. Jerome, "Life of St. Hilarion." *Catholic Encyclopedia.* www.newadvent.org/fathers/3003.htm.
11. Willibald, *The Life of St. Boniface,* translated by C.H. Talbot. Internet History Sourcebooks Project, Paul Halsall, editor. www.fordham.edu/halsall/basis/willibald-boniface.html.
12. Thomas of Celano, *The Life of St. Francis,* translated by David Burr. Internet History Sourcebooks Project, Paul Halsall, editor. www.fordham.edu/halsall/source/stfran-lives.html.
13. Quoted in Tony McAleavy, *Life in a Medieval Abbey.* New York: Enchanted Lion, 2003, p. 14.
14. St. Benedict, *Holy Rule.*

15. Quoted in The Cistercians in Yorkshire. http://cistercians.shef.ac.uk/glossary/novice-master.php.

16. Brian C. Taylor, "Stability, Obedience and Conversion of Life: A Benedictine Reflection on the Feast of the Holy Trinity," sermon on June 15, 2003, St. Michael and All Angels Episcopal Church. www.all-angels.com/sermontrinitybenedict20th.htm.

Chapter Two: A Life of Obedience

17. St. Benedict, *Holy Rule.*

18. Knowles, *Christian Monasticism,* p. 34.

19. St. Augustine of Hippo, *The Rule of St. Augustine.* Jack Pejza's Page. www.geocities.com/athens/1534/ruleaug.html#observance%20of%20the%20rule.

20. St. Benedict, *Holy Rule.*

21. St. Benedict, *Holy Rule.*

22. St. Benedict, *Holy Rule.*

23. St. Benedict, *Holy Rule.*

24. St. Benedict, *Holy Rule.*

25. St. Benedict, *Holy Rule.*

26. St. Benedict, *Holy Rule.*

27. St. Benedict, *Holy Rule.*

28. St. Benedict, *Holy Rule.*

29. St. Benedict, *Holy Rule.*

30. St. Benedict, *Holy Rule.*

Chapter Three: A Life of Work

31. St. Benedict, *Holy Rule.*

32. Francis of Assisi, *Rule of 1221 for the Friars Minor.* Early Franciscan Sources. www.nafra-sfo.org/work_commission_resources/wrkearly.html.

33. St. Benedict, *Holy Rule.*

34. St. Benedict, *Holy Rule.*

35. St. Benedict, *Holy Rule.*

36. Quoted in McAleavy, *Life in a Medieval Abbey,* p. 6.

37. Bernard of Clairvaux, *Apology,* translated by David Burr. Internet History Sourcebooks Project, Paul Halsall, editor. www.fordham.edu/halsall/source/bernard1.html.

38. Quoted in Otto von Simson, *The Gothic Cathedral.* New York: Pantheon, 1956, p. 100.

39. Quoted in Lynda McDaniel, "For the Glory of God." Beliefnet. www.beliefnet.com/story/11/story_1116_1.html.

Chapter Four: A Life of Prayer

40. Quoted in Knowles, *Christian Monasticism,* p. 18.

41. St. Benedict, *Holy Rule.*

42. St. Benedict, *Holy Rule.*

43. Quoted in "Lauds." *Catholic Encyclopedia.* www.newadvent.org/cathen/09038a.htm.

44. St. Benedict, *Holy Rule.*

45. St. Benedict, *Holy Rule.*

46. Quoted in Knowles, *Christian Monasticism,* p. 53.

47. St. Benedict, *Holy Rule.*

48. St. John Cassian, "Of the Method of Continual Prayer." Christian Classics

Ethereal Library. www.ccel.org/ccel/schaff/npnf211.iv.iv.xi.x. html.

49. St. Benedict, *Holy Rule.*
50. Quoted in Walter Nigg, *Warriors of God: The Great Religious Orders and Their Founders.* New York: Alfred A. Knopf, 1971, p. 99.

Chapter Five: A Life of Learning

51. St. Benedict, *Holy Rule.*
52. Hilary Thimmesh, "Benedictines and Higher Education American Style, Part I." Order of St. Benedict. www.osb.org/acad/thimmesh.html.
53. Quoted in Kevin Jones, "The Traditional History of the Ogham." The Nemeton of Taliere. http://members.tripod.com/taliere/ogham. htm.
54. Knowles, *Christian Monasticism,* p. 46.
55. Quoted in Daryl McCarthy, "Hearts and Minds Aflame for Christ: Medieval Irish Monks—A Model for Dynamic Learning and Living." International Institute for Christian Studies. www.iics.com/irishmonks. html.
56. Thomas Cahill, *How the Irish Saved Civilization.* New York: Nan A. Talese, 1995, p. 195.
57. Quoted in "Carolingian Schools." *Catholic Encyclopedia.* www.newadvent.org/cathen/03349c.htm.
58. Quoted in "Carolingian Schools."
59. Quoted in "Carolingian Schools."
60. Quote in Marjorie Rowling, *Every-day Life in Medieval Times.* New York: Dorset, 1968, p. 143.
61. Quoted in George Gordon Coulton, *Life in the Middle Ages.* Book IV. Cambridge, UK: Cambridge University Press, 1967, p. 102.
62. Quoted in George Gordon Coulton, *The Medieval Village.* New York: Dover, 1989, p. 265.
63. Quoted in Coulton, *Medieval Village,* p. 259.

Chapter Six: A Life of Valor

64. St. Bernard of Clairvaux, "On the New Knighthood," translated by Conrad Greenia. The Sovereign Military and Hospitaller Order of St. John of Jerusalem of Rhodes and of Malta. www.smom-za.org/ bgt/bgt_1_1.htm.
65. Jacques de Vitry, "Sermons to a Military Order," translated by Helen J. Nicholson. De re Militari: The Society for Medieval Military History. www.deremilitari.org/resources/sources/vitry.htm.
66. Quoted in Stephen Howarth, *The Knights Templar: Christian Chivalry and the Crusades, 1095–1314.* New York: Atheneum, 1992, p. 67.
67. Quoted in Howarth, *Knights Templar,* p. 55.
68. Quoted in "The Knights Templar." *Catholic Encyclopedia.* www.newadvent. org/cathen/14493a.htm.
69. Piers Paul Read, *The Templars.* New York: St. Martin's, 1999, p. 104.

Chapter Seven:
A Life of Service

70. Quoted in Nigg, *Warriors of God*, p. 220.
71. Quoted in Nigg, *Warriors of God*, p. 218.
72. Norman F. Cantor, *The Civilization of the Middle Ages*. New York: Harper-Collins, 1993, p. 433.
73. "The Primitive Constitution of the Order of Friars Preachers." Ordo Praedictorum. www.op.org/domcentral/trad/domdocs/0011.htm.
74. Cantor, *Civilization of the Middle Ages*, p. 440.
75. Andrew Joseph Munoz, "History of the Carmelites." Catholic Mystics. www.helpfellowship.org/carmelites.htm.

Chapter Eight:
A Life Unchanging

76. Brian Moynahan, *The Faith: A History of Christianity*. New York: Doubleday, 2002, p. 213.
77. Quoted in "St. Basil the Great." Congregation of St. Basil. www.basilian.org/Publica/StBasil/Stbasil4.htm.
78. Quoted in "Eastern Monasticism Before Chalcedon (A.D. 451)." *Catholic Encyclopedia*. www.newadvent.org/cathen/10464a.htm.
79. Quoted in "Eastern Monasticism."
80. St. Theodore of Studium, "Reform Rule," translated by A. Gardner. Internet History Sourcebooks Project, Paul Halsall, editor. www.fordham.edu/halsall/source/theostud-rules.html.
81. Knowles, *Christian Monasticism*, p. 126.

Epilogue:
Twilight and Legacy

82. Knowles, *Christian Monasticism*, p. 142.
83. Quoted in Lowell C. Green, "Change in Luther's Doctrine of the Ministry." Semper Reformanda: A Journal for Lutheran Reformation. http://members.aol.com/semperref/cjange.html.
84. Quoted in Peter G. Beidler, "Backgrounds to Chaucer." The Orb: On-Line Reference Book for Medieval Studies. www.the-orb.net/textbooks/anthology/beidler/clerics.html.
85. Quoted in Thomas E. Woods, *How the Catholic Church Built Western Civilization*. Washington, DC: Regnery, 2005, p. 45.
86. Knowles, *Christian Monasticism*, p. 244.

For Further Reading

Books

George Gordon Coulton, *Life in the Middle Ages*. Cambridge, UK: Cambridge University Press, 1967. A treasury of primary source excerpts on various topics. Originally a single volume, this version combines Books I and II in one binding and Books III and IV in a second.

Mark Galli, *Francis of Assisi and His World*. Downer's Grove, IL: InterVarsity 2002. A good introduction to understanding St. Francis and the spirituality of the Middle Ages.

Barbara A. Hanawalt, *The Middle Ages: An Illustrated History*. New York: Oxford University Press, 1998. Lavishly illustrated survey of the period, including subjects from architecture to warfare.

William W. Lace, *Christianity*. San Diego: Lucent, 2005. Part of the Great Religions of the World series, this book traces the history of Christianity from the time of the disciples of Jesus to the present.

Tony McAleavy, *Life in a Medieval Abbey*. New York: Enchanted Lion, 2003. Well-illustrated account of monastic life divided by topics and concentrating on development in the British Isles.

Walter Nigg, *Warriors of God: The Great Religious Orders and Their Founders*. New York: Alfred A. Knopf, 1971. Chapter-length profiles of the key figures in the history of monasticism, including Pachomius, Benedict, Basil, and several others.

Piers Paul Read, *The Templars*. New York: St. Martin's, 1999. Fascinating story of the Knights Templar with especially good introductory material and good color illustrations.

Victoria Sherrow, *Life in a Medieval Monastery*. San Diego: Lucent, 2000. Part of the series The Way People Live, this book gives a detailed and insightful look at the day-to-day life of monks.

Internet Sources

"The Ancient Templar Rule of Order," translated by Judith Upton-Ward. Ordo Supremus Militaris Templi Heirosolymintani. www.ordotempli. org/ancient-templar-rule-of-order. htm. Written in 1129, these rules served as a guide for the warrior monks known as Templars.

Athanasius of Alexandria, *Life of St. Antony*, translated by H. Ellershaw. Internet History Sourcebooks Project, Paul Halsall, editor. www.fordham.

edu/halsall/basis/vita-antony.html. A biography, written some time between 356 and 362, of the man widely considered to be the father of monasticism.

Rachel Gilberts, Middle Ages. www.mnsu.edu/emuseum/history/middleages. Fun to explore and extremely well illustrated site on the Middle Ages. Produced by Minnesota State University at Mankato.

Daryl McCarthy, "Hearts and Minds Aflame for Christ: Medieval Irish Monks—A Model for Dynamic Learning and Living." International Institute for Christian Studies. www.iics.com/irishmonks.html.

Middle Ages. www.learner.org/exhibits/middleages. Extensive site on different facets of Middle Ages culture produced by Annenberg CPB/Learner.Org.

NetSERF: The Internet Connection to the Middle Ages. www.netserf.org. Provides links to hundreds of aspects of life in the Middle Ages, including biographies, art, architecture, literature, and culture.

"St. Basil the Great." Congregation of St. Basil. www.basilian.org/Publica/Stbasil/Stbasil/index.htm. Four-part account of the life and work of the monk most responsible for the development of Eastern monasticism.

St. Benedict of Nursia, *The Holy Rule of St. Benedict*, translated by Boniface Verheyen. Christian Classics Ethereal Library. www.ccel.org/b/benedict/rule2/rule.html. Complete text of the rule that governed the lives and conduct of most monks and nuns in the Middle Ages.

Thomas of Celano, *The Life of St. Francis*, translated by David Burr. Internet History Sourcebooks Project, Paul Halsall, editor. www.fordham.edu/halsall/source/stfran-lives.html. Interesting account of the life of St. Francis by one of his close followers.

Thomas E. Woods, "What We Owe the Monks." Lew Rockwell.com. www.lewrockwell.com/woods/woods43.html. Good analysis of the overall contributions of monasticism.

Index

Picture Credits

Cover image: The Art Archive/Dagli Orti
akg-images, 9
akg-images/British Library, 82
akg-images/Orsi Battaglini, 28
akg-images/Pietro Baguzzi, 86
Alinari/Regione Umbria/Art Resource, NY, 70
Basilica di San Marco, Venice, Italy, Cameraphoto Arte Venezia/Bridgeman Art Library, 47
Bridgeman Art Library/Getty Images, 90
Erich Lessing/Art Resource, NY, 21, 31, 34, 56, 76–77, 80, 92
© Gianni Dagli Orti/CORBIS, 18
Giraudon/Bridgeman Art Library, 37, 38
HIP/Art Resource, NY, 23, 68
Kunsthistorisches Museum, Vienna, Austria/Bridgeman Art Library, 91

Mark A. Sampson, 10, 45, 61, 79
Mary Evans Picture Library, 40
Réunion des Musées Nationaux/ Art Resource, NY, 54–55, 64
San Miniato al Monte, Florence, Italy/Bridgeman Art Library, 15
© Sandro Vannini/CORBIS, 13, 71
Scala/Art Resource, NY, 25, 74
The Art Archive, 52
The Art Archive/Monastery of St. Catherine Sinai Egypt/Dagli Orti, 43
The Art Archive/Musee Conde Chantilly/Dagli Orti, 50
The Art Archive/Musee du Chateau de Versailles/Dagli Orti, 63
The Art Archive/Museo Tridentino Arte Sacra Trento/Dagli Orti, 73
Werner Forman/Art Resource, NY, 85

About the Author

William W. Lace is a native of Fort Worth, Texas, where he is executive assistant to the chancellor at Tarrant County College. He holds a bachelor's degree from Texas Christian University, a master's degree from East Texas State, and a doctorate from the University of North Texas. Before joining Tarrant County College, he was director of the news service at the University of Texas at Arlington and a writer and columnist for the *Fort Worth Star-Telegram*. He has written more than twenty-five books for Lucent, one of which—*The Death Camps*—was selected by the New York Public Library for its 1999 Recommended Teenage Reading List. He and his wife, Laura, a retired school librarian, live in Arlington, Texas, and have two children and three grandchildren.